Malta

Everything You Need

to Know

Introduction to Malta: A Mediterranean Jewel

Nestled in the heart of the Mediterranean Sea, Malta stands as a jewel of history, culture, and natural beauty. This tiny archipelago, consisting of three main islands—Malta, Gozo, and Comino—has a rich and diverse heritage that dates back millennia. Its strategic location at the crossroads of Europe, Africa, and the Middle East has made it a coveted prize for empires throughout history.

The story of Malta begins with its ancient origins, tracing its roots back to the Neolithic period, around 3600 BC. The earliest inhabitants left their mark in the form of megalithic temples, which still stand today as some of the world's oldest freestanding structures. These temples, such as Ħaġar Qim and Mnajdra, provide a window into the spiritual beliefs and architectural prowess of Malta's earliest settlers.

Over the centuries, Malta's location made it a magnet for various civilizations. The Phoenicians, Carthaginians, and Romans all left their imprints, contributing to the island's evolving culture and heritage. The Romans, in particular, made Malta an important naval base, using it as a key point in their Mediterranean conquests.

The Arab and Byzantine periods ushered in a new era of influence, with Arabic culture leaving an enduring impact on the Maltese language and way of life. The Byzantine Empire, too, held sway over Malta, marking another chapter in the island's complex history.

Perhaps the most iconic period in Malta's history is the era of the Knights of St. John, also known as the Knights Hospitaller. In 1530, the Knights arrived in Malta after being granted the islands by Emperor Charles V of Spain. Their rule saw the construction of Valletta, the fortified capital city that still stands today as a testament to their grand architectural vision. The Great Siege of 1565, where the Knights successfully defended Malta from an Ottoman invasion, remains a defining moment in Maltese history.

The modern era saw Malta under various foreign dominions, including the French and the British. British rule, which lasted for nearly 160 years, left an indelible mark on the island, influencing everything from its legal system to its education.

Malta's journey to independence culminated in 1964 when it became a sovereign nation. Since then, it has continued to evolve, embracing its unique blend of influences while forging its own identity in the modern world.

As we delve deeper into the chapters of this book, we'll explore Malta's geography, climate, flora, and fauna, all of which contribute to its remarkable natural beauty. We'll also delve into the intricacies of Maltese cuisine, renowned for its Mediterranean flavors and unique dishes.

But before we embark on this journey through Malta, it's essential to understand the historical tapestry that forms the backdrop of this Mediterranean jewel. From ancient temples to the Knights of St. John, from Arab influences to British colonial legacies, Malta's history is a mosaic of civilizations, each leaving a mark on this remarkable archipelago.

Malta's Ancient Origins

Malta's ancient origins trace back to a time long before recorded history, to an era when early humans first settled in this Mediterranean haven. The story of Malta's antiquity unfolds like a mystery, with archaeological evidence shedding light on its distant past.

Archaeological excavations have uncovered that the islands of Malta were inhabited as far back as the Neolithic period, approximately 3600 BC. This period is often referred to as the "Temple Period" due to the remarkable megalithic temples that dot the Maltese landscape. These temples, such as Ħaġar Qim, Mnajdra, and Tarxien, are some of the world's oldest free-standing structures, predating the Egyptian pyramids and Stonehenge by centuries.

The construction of these temples is a testament to the advanced engineering skills of Malta's early inhabitants. Massive limestone blocks, some weighing several tons, were carved and precisely fitted together to create these awe-inspiring religious sites. The purpose of these temples remains a subject of scholarly debate, with theories ranging from astronomical observatories to places of worship and community gatherings.

Malta's prehistoric people were skilled artisans, crafting intricate figurines, pottery, and ornaments. These artifacts provide valuable insights into their daily lives, beliefs, and social structures. The most famous of these artifacts is the "Venus of Malta," a small but exquisitely detailed figurine representing a woman, believed to be a symbol of fertility.

The temple builders of Malta were not limited to the main island; they also left their mark on the smaller islands of Gozo and Comino. Gozo's Ggantija Temples, a UNESCO World Heritage Site, are among the most ancient religious structures in the world.

Throughout the Neolithic period, Malta's inhabitants were primarily farmers and herders, relying on a subsistence economy. The abundance of archeological evidence, including tools and pottery, provides a glimpse into their daily lives and the resources they used.

The decline of the temple-building culture marked the end of the Neolithic period on Malta. The reasons behind this decline remain speculative, with factors such as environmental changes, social shifts, or external influences all being considered.

While much is still shrouded in mystery, one thing is certain: Malta's ancient origins represent a remarkable chapter in the island's history. The megalithic temples, sophisticated craftsmanship, and the enduring presence of these enigmatic structures serve as a testament to the ingenuity and resilience of Malta's early inhabitants. The echoes of their civilization still resonate through the millennia, connecting modern-day Malta with its awe-inspiring Neolithic past.

The Phoenician and Roman Influence

As we delve deeper into the annals of Malta's history, we come to a pivotal chapter marked by the influence of two great civilizations: the Phoenicians and the Romans. These ancient cultures left indelible marks on the Maltese archipelago, shaping its development in profound ways.

The Phoenicians, renowned as seafaring traders and explorers, arrived on Malta's shores around the 8th century BC. They established settlements on the islands, including on the main island of Malta and the smaller ones like Gozo and Comino. Malta's strategic location in the central Mediterranean made it an ideal stopover for Phoenician ships navigating the waters between their homeland in the eastern Mediterranean and their trading partners in the west.

One of the most significant Phoenician contributions to Malta was the introduction of their written script. The Maltese language itself bears traces of Phoenician influence, particularly in its earliest written inscriptions. This linguistic connection serves as a tangible reminder of the island's Phoenician heritage.

The Phoenicians also engaged in trade with the indigenous population, exchanging goods such as pottery, jewelry, and textiles. Archaeological discoveries, including Phoenician pottery fragments and jewelry, provide compelling evidence of this cultural interchange.

However, the Phoenician presence in Malta was not without its challenges. Malta's location also made it a coveted prize for various regional powers, and the islands experienced periods of instability and conquest. The Carthaginians, who shared Phoenician roots, established control over Malta after the fall of Phoenician power. This marked another chapter in the island's complex history.

In 218 BC, the Romans set their sights on Malta, and the islands fell under Roman rule during the Punic Wars. The Roman influence on Malta was profound and enduring. They brought with them the Latin language, which would lay the foundation for the development of the Maltese language as we know it today.

Under Roman rule, Malta prospered. The Romans recognized the strategic importance of the islands and invested in infrastructure, including roads, aqueducts, and fortifications. The ancient city of Melite, known today as Mdina, was a thriving Roman urban center.

The introduction of Christianity to Malta during the Roman period was another pivotal moment. The apostle St. Paul is said to have been shipwrecked on the island in 60 AD while en route to Rome, and this event is a significant part of Maltese Christian tradition.

The enduring Roman legacy is evident in the numerous archaeological sites and Roman-era artifacts that have been unearthed on Malta. The Roman Villa at Rabat, the catacombs of St. Paul, and the Roman townhouse in Rabat are just a few examples of the tangible remnants of this ancient influence.

As we explore Malta's historical tapestry, the Phoenician and Roman chapters stand as testament to the island's resilience and adaptability in the face of changing civilizations. Their contributions, whether linguistic, architectural, or cultural, continue to shape Malta's identity to this day, adding depth and richness to its captivating story.

The Arab and Byzantine Periods

In the intricate tapestry of Malta's history, the Arab and Byzantine periods stand as significant threads, weaving together a narrative of cultural exchange and transformation. These periods brought new influences to the islands, leaving an indelible mark on Malta's identity.

The Arab period in Malta's history commenced in the 9th century AD, when Arab forces from North Africa swept across the Mediterranean, seeking to extend their dominion. Malta's strategic location made it a target, and the Arab rulers, who brought with them a rich cultural heritage, established control over the islands.

During this time, Malta experienced a blending of cultures, with Arabic influences leaving a lasting impact. The most visible testament to this influence can be seen in the Maltese language itself. Arabic words and phrases found their way into the Maltese lexicon, enriching the island's linguistic diversity. Even today, many Maltese words bear traces of their Arabic origins, serving as a linguistic bridge to this period of history.

The Arab rulers also made significant contributions to Malta's agriculture. They introduced new crops and irrigation techniques that enhanced agricultural productivity. This agricultural legacy shaped Malta's landscape, contributing to its lush greenery and terraced fields.

However, the Arab period was not without its challenges. Malta's history during this time is marked by a degree of instability and conflict as various powers sought control over the islands. It was during the Arab rule that the Byzantine Empire, with its capital in Constantinople (modern-day Istanbul), sought to assert its authority.

The Byzantine influence on Malta was marked by efforts to bring the islands under their control. The Maltese islands became part of the Byzantine Exarchate of Carthage, a Byzantine administrative division that oversaw North Africa and the western Mediterranean.

The Byzantines left their mark on Malta's administration, with a structured governance system that reflected their bureaucratic prowess. The remnants of Byzantine-era buildings and fortifications serve as a tangible reminder of their presence.

One of the enduring legacies of the Byzantine period was the spread of Christianity. The Byzantines promoted Christianity on the islands, and numerous churches and religious sites dating from this period still stand today, testifying to the enduring faith of the Maltese people.

As we reflect on the Arab and Byzantine periods, we witness Malta's ability to absorb and adapt to the changing tides of history. These periods of cultural exchange enriched the island's heritage, leaving an imprint on its language, agriculture, and religious traditions. They are yet another chapter in Malta's storied past, a testament to its resilience and capacity to embrace diversity while forging its own unique identity in the Mediterranean.

The Knights of St. John and Their Legacy

In the grand narrative of Malta's history, few chapters shine as brightly as the era of the Knights of St. John. This remarkable period left an indelible legacy on the Maltese islands, shaping their culture, architecture, and identity in profound ways.

The Knights of St. John, formally known as the Knights Hospitaller of St. John of Jerusalem, arrived in Malta in 1530. Prior to their arrival, the knights had faced trials and tribulations, having been displaced from their original home in the Holy Land during the Crusades. Their journey eventually led them to Malta, which they were granted by Emperor Charles V of Spain in recognition of their service and valor.

Upon their arrival, the Knights wasted no time in fortifying the island. Their crowning achievement was the construction of Valletta, the fortified capital city that still stands today as a testament to their architectural vision. The city, designed by the renowned architect Francesco Laparelli, became a masterpiece of military engineering, earning it the nickname "The Fortress City."

The Knights' rule over Malta saw the island flourish economically, as they encouraged trade and commerce. They also strengthened Malta's defenses, understanding the strategic importance of the archipelago. One of the most defining moments in Malta's history occurred in 1565 when the Knights successfully defended the island against a massive Ottoman invasion during the Great Siege of Malta. This heroic resistance solidified the Knights' place in Maltese hearts and history.

Under the Knights' rule, Malta became a hub of culture and art, with the Order attracting scholars, artists, and craftsmen from across Europe. This cultural fusion left a lasting impact on Malta's identity, as seen in its art, architecture, and traditions.

The legacy of the Knights extends to religion as well. They were fervently dedicated to their Catholic faith, and their influence bolstered Malta's deeply rooted religious traditions. Churches and chapels dedicated to various saints still dot the landscape, serving as spiritual and architectural treasures.

The Knights' legacy on Malta endured even after their departure. In 1798, Napoleon Bonaparte's forces invaded the island, leading to the Knights' expulsion. Yet, their memory and the enduring imprint they left behind continue to shape Malta's cultural and historical narrative.

As we reflect on the era of the Knights of St. John, we witness a chapter in Malta's history marked by valor, architectural splendor, and cultural enrichment. Their legacy is etched into the very fabric of the islands, reminding us of their enduring impact on Malta's past and present. It's a legacy that continues to captivate those who explore the fortified streets of Valletta and delve into the rich history of the Maltese archipelago.

Malta in the Modern Era

The modern era in Malta's history is a story of transformation, adaptation, and the island nation's journey toward independence and self-determination. It's a tale of political changes, economic shifts, and a resilient people who have navigated the challenges of the 20th and 21st centuries with determination.

Following the departure of the Knights of St. John in the late 18th century, Malta found itself under French control briefly before becoming part of the British Empire in 1814, a status that would endure for nearly 160 years. British rule brought about significant changes to Malta's governance, infrastructure, and society. The British introduced English as an official language alongside Maltese, leaving a lasting impact on the island's linguistic landscape.

During World War II, Malta played a crucial role as a strategic naval and air base. The island endured relentless bombings and hardships but ultimately emerged as a symbol of resilience and defiance. In recognition of its wartime valor, King George VI awarded the George Cross to Malta in 1942, making it the only entire nation to receive such an honor.

The post-war period saw Malta's political landscape evolve. The push for self-determination and independence gained momentum, leading to constitutional changes and negotiations with the British government. In 1964, Malta achieved its goal of becoming a sovereign nation within the British Commonwealth. Malta's path to independence paved the way for further progress in the latter half of the

20th century. The island nation invested in education, healthcare, and infrastructure, fostering economic growth and development. Tourism also became a significant driver of the economy, drawing visitors with its historical sites, picturesque landscapes, and Mediterranean charm.

In 1971, Malta adopted a republican constitution, and in 1974, it officially became a republic, severing its remaining ties to the British monarchy. The 1980s brought about significant political changes, with the rise of the Malta Labour Party, which advocated for further social and economic reforms.

In the 21st century, Malta continued to evolve as a member of the European Union since 2004, further solidifying its place on the global stage. The country's economy diversified, with sectors like finance and iGaming experiencing rapid growth. The attractive tax incentives for foreign businesses and individuals contributed to Malta's emergence as an international business hub.

However, Malta also faced challenges, including issues related to governance, corruption, and immigration. These challenges prompted important discussions and reforms as the country worked to address these issues and strengthen its institutions.

Today, Malta stands as a modern European nation with a rich historical heritage. Its vibrant culture, stunning landscapes, and thriving economy make it a destination that continues to captivate visitors and residents alike. As Malta strides into the future, it does so with a sense of pride in its history and a determination to forge a bright and prosperous path ahead.

Malta's Road to Independence

The road to independence for Malta was marked by a journey of political evolution, social change, and the tireless efforts of its people. It was a path that spanned centuries, ultimately culminating in the achievement of full sovereignty in the mid-20th century.

The British Empire's presence in Malta, which began in 1814, brought with it a series of constitutional changes that would set the stage for Malta's quest for independence. Initially, British rule was met with mixed reactions, with some segments of Maltese society welcoming the stability and economic opportunities it provided, while others chafed under colonial control.

One of the key turning points in Malta's journey toward independence was the adoption of a more representative constitution in 1887. This Constitution granted a degree of self-government and introduced a legislative council, allowing Maltese elected representatives to have a say in local affairs. However, real power still rested with the British colonial authorities.

The early 20th century witnessed a growing demand for greater autonomy and political rights. Malta's participation in World War I, alongside British forces, heightened the island's sense of national identity and its desire for self-determination.

The interwar period brought about political turbulence, as the Maltese people pushed for constitutional reforms and further self-governance. The 1921 Constitution, known as the "Malta Letters Patent," granted Malta a higher degree of self-governance, with the establishment of a bicameral legislature.

However, political tensions persisted, and the power balance between the British colonial administration and the Maltese political leaders remained a point of contention. World War II brought Malta into the global spotlight as the island endured intense bombing by Axis forces. The bravery and resilience of the Maltese people during the war earned them international recognition and admiration. In 1942, King George VI awarded the George Cross to Malta for its "heroic deeds and bravery."

The post-war period saw Malta's push for self-determination gain momentum. The 1947 Constitution granted Malta internal self-government with a measure of autonomy in domestic affairs. However, key issues, including defense and foreign affairs, remained under British control.

Political leaders like George Borg Olivier and Dom Mintoff played instrumental roles in the negotiations for Malta's independence. The Malta Integration Act of 1956 aimed to unite Malta with Britain, but the plan faced opposition and was ultimately abandoned in favor of full independence.

On September 21, 1964, Malta achieved its long-sought goal of independence from Britain and became a sovereign nation within the British Commonwealth. This marked the culmination of years of political struggle, negotiation, and the determination of the Maltese people to chart their own course in history.

Malta's road to independence was marked by a complex interplay of political, social, and historical factors. It was a journey of self-discovery and a testament to the resilience and spirit of a nation that sought to shape its destiny on the global stage. Independence was not the end but the beginning of a new chapter in Malta's history, one that continues to unfold in the 21st century.

Malta's Unique Geography and Climate

The geography of Malta, nestled in the heart of the Mediterranean Sea, is nothing short of captivating. This small archipelago, consisting of three main islands—Malta, Gozo, and Comino—boasts a distinctive landscape shaped by millennia of natural processes. Add to this its Mediterranean climate, and you have a setting that is both unique and enchanting.

Let's start with Malta's geography. Located approximately 50 miles south of Sicily, Malta's strategic position has made it a coveted prize for empires throughout history. The islands are characterized by rocky coastlines, picturesque harbors, and rugged terrain, creating a dramatic and visually striking environment. The limestone formations, known as Globigerina limestone, dominate the landscape, lending a warm, golden hue to the buildings and cliffs that line the shores.

Valletta, the capital city, stands as a testament to Malta's geography. Perched on a hilly peninsula, it offers stunning panoramic views of the surrounding harbors and the sea beyond. The fortified city, with its labyrinthine streets, is a UNESCO World Heritage Site, celebrated for its architectural and historical significance.

Gozo, Malta's sister island, offers a contrasting landscape. It is known for its rolling hills, fertile valleys, and a sense of tranquility that sets it apart from the bustling energy of Malta. The stunning Azure Window, a natural limestone arch that tragically collapsed in 2017, was once one of Gozo's most iconic geological features.

Comino, the smallest of the three islands, is a haven of natural beauty. It is largely uninhabited and known for the crystal-clear waters of the Blue Lagoon, which attract visitors from around the world.

The Maltese islands are also characterized by a Mediterranean climate, which is marked by hot, dry summers and mild, wet winters. Summers are long and generally rain-free, with temperatures often exceeding 30°C (86°F). The sea plays a crucial role in moderating the climate, with the surrounding waters helping to keep temperatures relatively stable.

Winters are mild and comfortable, with temperatures rarely dropping below 10°C (50°F). While rainfall occurs predominantly during the winter months, it is relatively low in quantity, making water a precious resource on the islands. Malta's unique geography also means that it can be susceptible to strong winds, especially in the winter months.

The combination of Malta's geography and climate has contributed to the development of a unique ecosystem, characterized by a variety of plant and animal species adapted to the island's arid conditions. The maquis, a Mediterranean shrubland, covers much of the islands and is home to a diverse range of flora and fauna, including indigenous species like the Maltese Wall Lizard.

In summation, Malta's geography and climate are integral to its identity. Its rocky coastlines, limestone formations, and Mediterranean climate create a picturesque and inviting setting that has charmed travelers and residents for centuries. Understanding these natural features provides a deeper appreciation of Malta's rich history and its enduring allure as a Mediterranean jewel.

Flora and Fauna of the Maltese Islands

The Maltese Islands, with their unique geography and Mediterranean climate, host a diverse array of flora and fauna that have adapted to the challenges and opportunities of this distinctive environment. Exploring the natural world of Malta, Gozo, and Comino reveals a rich tapestry of life, with each species playing a vital role in this fragile ecosystem.

Let's begin with the flora. Malta's terrain, characterized by rocky landscapes and low rainfall, has given rise to a variety of hardy plant species. The maquis, a type of Mediterranean shrubland, blankets large portions of the islands. It's home to an assortment of resilient plants such as the Maltese Rock Centaury, Maltese Sea Lavender, and Maltese Everlasting, each uniquely adapted to the arid conditions.

Olive groves are a common sight across the islands, a testament to the enduring importance of olive cultivation in Maltese agriculture. Carob trees, with their distinct pods, also thrive in this climate, contributing to both traditional cuisine and local industries.

Gozo, with its more fertile soil and greener landscapes, supports a broader range of flora. Here, you'll find fields of wildflowers, including vibrant poppies and delicate daisies, adding splashes of color to the rolling hills.

Turning to the fauna, the Maltese Islands host a surprisingly diverse range of animal life. Birdwatchers, in particular, are drawn to Malta as a migration hotspot. The islands are situated along several major bird migration routes, making them a temporary home to numerous species during their travels. Birdwatchers may spot raptors like honey buzzards, marsh harriers, and kestrels, as well as songbirds such as warblers and finches.

The cliffs and rocky coastlines provide nesting sites for seabirds like Yellow-legged Gulls and Cory's Shearwaters. The surrounding waters are teeming with marine life, making Malta a popular destination for diving and snorkeling enthusiasts. The crystal-clear Mediterranean waters reveal a vibrant underwater world inhabited by colorful fish, octopuses, sea turtles, and even dolphins.

One unique and endangered species found exclusively in the Maltese Islands is the Maltese freshwater crab (Potamon fluviatile lanfrancoi). This small crab is native to a few isolated freshwater springs and streams on Malta and Gozo, making it a precious and protected species.

Land-based mammals in Malta are limited, with the rabbit being one of the few native species. However, the islands are home to a variety of reptiles, including the Maltese Wall Lizard, which has adapted to the limestone terrain.

The flora and fauna of the Maltese Islands provide a window into the intricate relationship between nature and the environment. These resilient species have adapted to the challenging conditions of this Mediterranean archipelago, demonstrating the remarkable ability of life to thrive in even the most inhospitable of landscapes. Exploring Malta's natural world is an opportunity to appreciate the delicate balance that sustains these islands and to marvel at the beauty and diversity of life in this unique Mediterranean setting.

Maltese Cuisine: A Taste of the Mediterranean

Malta's rich culinary tradition is a delicious fusion of Mediterranean flavors and influences that have shaped the island's gastronomy over centuries. This unique cuisine reflects the history, culture, and geography of the Maltese Islands, offering a tantalizing journey for food enthusiasts.

The Mediterranean Sea, with its bounty of fresh seafood, has played a central role in Maltese cuisine. Fish like lampuki (dolphin fish), swordfish, and octopus are staples in Maltese dishes. One beloved Maltese specialty is "Fenkata," a hearty rabbit stew cooked with wine, garlic, and herbs, showcasing the island's game traditions.

Mediterranean vegetables like tomatoes, olives, and capers feature prominently in Maltese cooking. The famous "Kapunata" is Malta's version of ratatouille, a savory dish combining these vegetables with garlic, herbs, and sometimes anchovies. It's a flavorful side dish or condiment that complements many Maltese meals.

Bread holds a special place in Maltese hearts and stomachs. "Hobz biz-zejt" is a popular Maltese sandwich featuring a thick slice of crusty bread soaked in olive oil and filled with tomatoes, capers, olives, and tuna. It's a simple yet delicious snack.

Malta's love affair with pasta is evident in dishes like "Pastizzi." These savory pastries are filled with either ricotta cheese or mushy peas and are a ubiquitous street food. "Timpana," a baked pasta dish with macaroni, minced meat, and a tomato sauce, is another comfort food favorite.

When it comes to sweets, Malta offers a delightful array of treats. "Kannoli" is a beloved dessert, consisting of fried pastry tubes filled with sweet ricotta cream, chocolate chips, and candied fruit. "Qubbajt," a sugary and nutty nougat, is another sweet delight often enjoyed during festivals.

Maltese cuisine also reflects its historical ties to various Mediterranean cultures. The Arab influence is evident in dishes like "Imqarrun il-Forn," a baked macaroni dish with béchamel sauce, reminiscent of Italian and Middle Eastern cuisines. "Sfineg," a type of fritter, has its roots in the Sicilian "sfinci" and is a favorite snack during the carnival season.

Wine production has a long history in Malta, with indigenous grape varieties such as "Gellewza" and "Ġirgentina" contributing to unique Maltese wines. The sweet dessert wine known as "Moscatel" is a local favorite.

Maltese cuisine is not just about the food but also the communal spirit of sharing meals. It's customary to enjoy meals with family and friends, celebrating life's moments with laughter, conversation, and delicious dishes.

In sum, Maltese cuisine is a testament to the island's rich history and vibrant culture. It's a culinary journey through time, blending the influences of Mediterranean civilizations into a tapestry of flavors that delight the senses and leave a lasting impression on those fortunate enough to savor its treasures.

Wines of Malta: A Hidden Delight

When one thinks of Mediterranean wines, places like Italy, France, and Spain often come to mind, stealing the spotlight with their renowned vineyards and centuries-old winemaking traditions. Yet, hidden amidst the azure waters of the Mediterranean lies a wine-producing gem that deserves a place in the sun: the wines of Malta.

Malta's winemaking history stretches back over 2,000 years, making it one of the oldest wine-producing regions in the world. Its unique terroir, marked by sun-drenched hillsides, rocky terrain, and the tempering influence of the Mediterranean Sea, creates an environment where grapevines thrive.

Indigenous grape varieties like "Gellewza" and "Girgentina" are the heart and soul of Maltese wines. Gellewza, a red grape, imparts rich, fruity flavors to the wines, while Girgentina, a white grape, contributes to crisp and aromatic whites. These grape varieties have adapted to Malta's climate and soil, resulting in wines that are uniquely Maltese.

One of Malta's wine treasures is the "Girgentina" grape, used to produce refreshing and aromatic white wines. This grape variety, often blended with other native grapes, brings citrus and floral notes to the glass. The best expressions of Girgentina come from the scenic valleys of Malta and Gozo, where the vines bask in the Mediterranean sun. Another noteworthy grape is the "Gellewza," which is primarily responsible for Maltese red wines. These wines exhibit a rich and full-bodied character, often with notes of dark fruits, spices, and a subtle hint of Mediterranean herbs. Gellewza wines are perfect companions for hearty Maltese dishes like rabbit stew and beef.

Among the hidden gems of Maltese winemaking is the sweet dessert wine known as "Moscatel." Made from the Muscat grape, this wine showcases the island's ability to produce exceptional sweet wines. The Muscat grape, grown in the sun-soaked vineyards, delivers intoxicating aromas of orange blossom, apricots, and honey, making it a perfect pairing with Maltese pastries like Kannoli or Qubbajt.

The wine industry in Malta has undergone a revival in recent decades. Modern winemakers have embraced innovative techniques while honoring traditional methods to produce high-quality wines that capture the essence of the Maltese terroir. Boutique wineries, like those in the charming region of Gozo, are garnering international recognition for their dedication to quality and the use of indigenous grape varieties.

Visiting Malta provides a unique opportunity to explore its winemaking heritage. Wine tours and tastings at local vineyards offer a chance to savor the flavors of Maltese wines while learning about the history and craftsmanship behind each bottle.

In conclusion, Malta's wines may be a hidden delight in the world of oenology, but they shine brightly with their distinctive flavors and rich history. These wines, crafted from ancient grape varieties in a sun-drenched Mediterranean paradise, are a testament to the enduring art of winemaking and a delightful discovery for wine enthusiasts willing to venture off the beaten path.

Exploring Malta's Stunning Coastlines

Malta's coastline is a masterpiece of nature's artistry, a tapestry of rugged cliffs, pristine beaches, and crystal-clear waters that captivate the senses and beckon adventurers to explore its beauty. This Mediterranean jewel boasts a coastline that offers a treasure trove of experiences for those willing to embark on a coastal journey.

Let's begin with the dramatic cliffs that adorn Malta's shores. The Dingli Cliffs, located on the southwestern coast of Malta, are some of the highest cliffs in Europe, rising 253 meters (830 feet) above sea level. Standing atop these majestic cliffs, you're treated to breathtaking panoramic views of the Mediterranean, where the azure waters stretch as far as the eye can see.

Comino, the smallest of Malta's islands, is home to the iconic Blue Lagoon, a natural wonder renowned for its crystal-clear waters and vibrant marine life. Visitors can swim, snorkel, or simply bask in the sun on the rocky shores, immersing themselves in a world of aquatic splendor.

For those seeking tranquility, Malta offers a plethora of secluded coves and hidden bays. Ghajn Tuffieha Bay, nestled between rugged cliffs and surrounded by lush vegetation, is a prime example. Its unspoiled beauty makes it a favored spot for sunbathing and swimming in pristine waters. The coastline is also adorned with historic treasures. The walled city of Valletta, a UNESCO World

Heritage Site, boasts an enchanting waterfront known as the Valletta Waterfront. Here, centuries-old buildings have been transformed into vibrant shops, restaurants, and cafes, offering a unique blend of history and modernity. Malta's coastal towns and villages, like Marsaxlokk, provide glimpses into traditional Mediterranean life. The colorful fishing boats that dot the harbors, known as "luzzu," are not only picturesque but also carry centuries of maritime heritage.

Gozo, with its more tranquil pace of life, offers coastal gems like Ramla Bay, known for its red-golden sands and crystal-clear waters. The towering Calypso's Cave, perched high above the coastline, is said to be the legendary home of the nymph Calypso in Homer's "The Odyssey."

Malta's coastlines are not just about natural beauty but also rich maritime history. The harbors of Marsamxett and Grand Harbour in Valletta have played pivotal roles in Mediterranean trade and warfare for centuries, with fortifications and historic buildings that stand as silent witnesses to the island's maritime past.

Exploring Malta's coastlines isn't limited to land-based adventures. The surrounding waters offer world-class diving and snorkeling opportunities, with underwater caves, reefs, and shipwrecks waiting to be explored by diving enthusiasts.

In conclusion, Malta's coastlines are a treasure trove of natural wonders, historical treasures, and opportunities for relaxation and adventure. Whether you're gazing from dramatic cliffs, lounging on a sandy beach, or diving into the deep blue, Malta's coastlines invite you to experience the Mediterranean's beauty in all its splendor.

Historic Capital: Valletta

Valletta, the jewel of the Mediterranean, stands as a living testament to Malta's rich history and enduring charm. This fortified city, perched on a rocky peninsula overlooking the sea, encapsulates centuries of stories, conquests, and cultural influences.

Named after Jean Parisot de Valette, the Grand Master of the Knights of St. John who defended Malta during the Great Siege of 1565, Valletta was conceived as a formidable fortress city. Its construction, which began in 1566 under the guidance of the architect Francesco Laparelli, was a monumental undertaking that resulted in a masterpiece of military engineering.

The city's grid layout, featuring narrow streets that wind their way uphill, was designed not only for aesthetics but also for defense. The limestone buildings, with their distinctive honey-colored facades, create a harmonious and visually striking urban landscape. Valletta's historic core, with its 320 historic monuments, earned it a UNESCO World Heritage Site designation.

One of the city's most iconic landmarks is St. John's Co-Cathedral, a baroque masterpiece that houses the famed Caravaggio painting, "The Beheading of Saint John the Baptist." The interior of the cathedral, adorned with intricate marble work, gilded sculptures, and a dazzling floor of inlaid marble tombstones, is a testament to the opulence of the Knights of St. John. Valletta's historic significance extends beyond its architecture. It has played pivotal roles in global history, from its defense against the

Ottoman Empire in 1565 to its strategic importance during World War II. During the war, the city endured intense bombing, with the resilience of its people earning Valletta the George Cross, a prestigious British award for bravery.

The Grand Harbour, flanked by Valletta's fortified walls, has long been a strategic maritime hub. It has witnessed the passage of naval fleets and merchant vessels, shaping the island's destiny. Fort St. Angelo and Fort St. Elmo, guarding the harbor's entrance, are enduring symbols of Malta's military heritage.

Yet, Valletta is not merely a museum frozen in time. It's a living, breathing city with a vibrant cultural scene. Its streets are adorned with art galleries, theaters, and open-air cafes where locals and visitors gather to savor life's pleasures.

The city is also home to the Grand Master's Palace, a historic building that now houses the Office of the President of Malta and the National Museum of Archaeology. This museum displays artifacts dating back to Malta's prehistoric period, providing insights into the island's ancient history.

Valletta's history, culture, and architectural splendor continue to draw travelers from around the world. As you wander through its narrow streets, you can't help but feel the weight of centuries and the enduring spirit of a city that has weathered storms, both literal and metaphorical. Valletta is more than a capital; it's a living embodiment of Malta's past and present, a city that invites you to explore its secrets and immerse yourself in its rich tapestry of history and culture.

Mdina: The Silent City

Nestled in the heart of Malta, atop a hill that seems to touch the heavens, lies Mdina, a city steeped in history and shrouded in a sense of timelessness. Known as "The Silent City," Mdina is a place where the past and present merge seamlessly, creating an atmosphere of tranquility and mystery.

The history of Mdina dates back over 4,000 years, making it one of Europe's oldest inhabited cities. It was founded by the Phoenicians and later inhabited by the Romans, Arabs, Normans, and Knights of St. John, each leaving their indelible mark on its character and architecture.

Entering Mdina feels like stepping back in time. The city's well-preserved medieval walls, constructed by the Arabs in the 9th century, create a sense of stepping into a different era. These fortified walls, made of honey-colored limestone, rise majestically above the surrounding landscape, offering breathtaking views of the Maltese countryside and the Mediterranean Sea.

Walking through Mdina's narrow, winding streets is like navigating a labyrinth of history. The architecture is a blend of medieval and Baroque styles, with elegant palaces, churches, and townhouses adorned with intricately carved balconies and doorways. One of the city's architectural gems is St. Paul's Cathedral, a stunning Baroque masterpiece that houses exquisite artworks and intricate frescoes.

Mdina's nickname, "The Silent City," reflects its unique ambiance. The absence of cars within its fortified walls contributes to the city's serenity. Visitors are greeted by the gentle echo of footsteps on cobblestone streets and the whisper of the wind through narrow alleys. It's a place where time seems to slow down, inviting contemplation and reflection.

The city has also played a role in the world of entertainment. Mdina served as a filming location for various movies and television series, most notably "Game of Thrones," where it stood in as the fictional city of King's Landing.

Mdina's history is intertwined with tales of knights, nobility, and intrigue. The city was home to several noble families and played a pivotal role during the Knights of St. John's rule. The city's medieval dungeons, part of the Palazzo Falson Historic House, provide a chilling glimpse into its past.

Today, Mdina is not merely a relic of the past but a vibrant city with a thriving community. It houses cafes, restaurants, and boutique shops where visitors can savor Maltese cuisine, sip coffee in historic squares, and explore the intricate craftsmanship of local artisans.

Mdina is a city of contrasts, where ancient and modern coexist harmoniously. It's a place where the walls speak of centuries gone by, where the breeze carries whispers of history, and where every step is a journey through time. To experience Mdina is to immerse oneself in the timeless beauty of Malta's heritage, a city that invites you to listen to the echoes of history and savor the serenity of "The Silent City."

Sliema and St. Julian's: Modern Maltese Marvels

Nestled along Malta's northeastern coastline, the neighboring towns of Sliema and St. Julian's have evolved into vibrant hubs of contemporary life, offering a modern contrast to the island's ancient history. These bustling locales have become dynamic centers of commerce, leisure, and entertainment while preserving a connection to their picturesque Mediterranean roots.

Sliema, whose name derives from the Maltese word for "peace," has indeed become a peaceful haven for residents and visitors alike. Its iconic promenade, known as the Sliema Front, stretches along the coast, offering stunning views of Valletta's historic skyline across the harbor. A leisurely stroll along this promenade is a delightful way to soak in the Mediterranean ambiance.

The heart of Sliema is lined with a blend of historic townhouses and modern apartments, providing a glimpse into Malta's architectural diversity. Sliema is also a shopping paradise, with streets like Bisazza Street and Tower Road featuring a mix of international brands and local boutiques. St. Julian's, or "San Ġiljan" in Maltese, is adjacent to Sliema and is known for its bustling nightlife and entertainment. The picturesque Spinola Bay is a focal point, with colorful fishing boats bobbing in the harbor and a myriad of restaurants and bars lining the waterfront. Paceville, a district within St. Julian's, is the heart of Malta's nightlife scene. It comes alive after dark, with a wide array of clubs, bars, and entertainment venues catering to diverse tastes. Whether you're seeking a quiet evening by the sea or a night of dancing and music, St. Julian's has something to offer.

Both Sliema and St. Julian's boast a thriving culinary scene. The diverse restaurants in these towns cater to a wide range of tastes, from traditional Maltese dishes to international cuisine. Seafood restaurants are particularly popular, offering the freshest catches of the day.

The towns are also home to several cultural and entertainment venues, including theaters, cinemas, and art galleries. The Manoel Theatre, one of Europe's oldest working theaters, is located in the heart of Sliema and hosts a variety of performances throughout the year.

A highlight of this area is the opportunity for watersports and outdoor activities. Sliema and St. Julian's offer easy access to diving, snorkeling, and boat trips to explore the surrounding coastline and crystal-clear waters. The bustling harbors also serve as departure points for ferry services to explore other parts of Malta and the neighboring islands.

Both towns have seen a significant influx of expatriates and tourists, contributing to a cosmopolitan atmosphere. English is widely spoken, and many international companies have established a presence in the area, making it a hub for business and commerce.

In summary, Sliema and St. Julian's are modern Maltese marvels that beautifully balance the past and present. These towns offer a blend of history, culture, entertainment, and leisure, making them dynamic destinations for those looking to experience Malta's contemporary side while savoring the Mediterranean lifestyle.

The Three Cities: Birgu, Senglea, and Cospicua

Nestled on the southeastern coast of Malta, the Three Cities—Birgu, Senglea, and Cospicua—stand as living monuments to Malta's maritime history and enduring resilience. These fortified towns, often referred to as the "Cottonera," are a testament to the island's strategic significance in the Mediterranean.

Birgu, also known as Vittoriosa, is the oldest of the Three Cities, with a history dating back to Phoenician times. Its name, "Birgu," means "city of the knights," a nod to its role as the Knights of St. John's first headquarters when they arrived in Malta in 1530. The city's narrow, winding streets are lined with historic buildings, churches, and palaces, reflecting its rich heritage.

One of Birgu's most iconic landmarks is Fort St. Angelo, a formidable fortress that has witnessed numerous sieges and battles over the centuries. It played a pivotal role in the Great Siege of 1565 when the Knights of St. John defended Malta from the Ottoman Empire.

Senglea, or Isla in Maltese, is a town located on a small peninsula adjacent to Birgu. Its name is derived from Grand Master Claude de la Sengle, who fortified the town in the 16th century. Senglea's narrow streets and quaint squares evoke a sense of old-world charm. The Gardjola Gardens, perched on the tip of the peninsula, offer panoramic views of the Grand Harbour and are adorned with the iconic "Gardjola," a stone watchtower adorned with the symbols of peace and watchfulness.

Cospicua, also known as Bormla, is the largest of the Three Cities and is situated between Birgu and Senglea. Its history is intertwined with shipbuilding and maritime trade, and remnants of its industrial past can still be seen along the waterfront. Cospicua's streets are lined with churches, baroque architecture, and bustling markets, providing a glimpse into the daily life of its residents.

The Grand Harbour, flanked by these three towns, has been a key to Malta's maritime prominence. The natural harbor, one of the finest in the Mediterranean, has served as a safe haven for fleets, merchant vessels, and warships throughout history. The strategically located Fort Ricasoli, guarding the entrance to the harbor, has played a vital role in protecting Malta from invasions.

The Three Cities have not only borne witness to history but have also contributed to it. During World War II, the towns endured heavy bombing by Axis forces, earning them the George Cross for the resilience and bravery of their people.

Today, the Three Cities offer a captivating blend of history, culture, and community. The restoration of historic buildings and waterfront promenades has breathed new life into these towns, attracting visitors who seek to immerse themselves in Malta's maritime past and explore the quaint streets and picturesque views.

In summary, the Three Cities—Birgu, Senglea, and Cospicua—represent a living chronicle of Malta's maritime heritage. These fortified towns, with their historic architecture, vibrant communities, and strategic significance, offer a journey through time, inviting visitors to step into the footsteps of knights, sailors, and the resilient people who have called these towns home for centuries.

Gozo: Malta's Sister Island

Lying just a short ferry ride north of the main island of Malta, Gozo is a Mediterranean gem that often goes unnoticed by travelers eager to explore its larger sibling. But those who venture to this serene sister island discover a place of unique beauty, rich history, and a pace of life that feels like a step back in time.

Gozo is the second-largest of the Maltese archipelago's islands, and it offers a striking contrast to the bustling streets of Malta. With a population that's a fraction of its larger neighbor and an area of just 67 square kilometers (26 square miles), Gozo embodies tranquility and simplicity.

The island's name, Gozo, is believed to be derived from the Maltese word "ghawdex," which means "joy." And indeed, Gozo is a place that brings joy to those who visit, thanks to its breathtaking landscapes, crystal-clear waters, and a way of life that celebrates nature and tradition.

One of the island's most iconic landmarks is the Azure Window, a natural limestone arch that once stood as a testament to nature's artistry. Unfortunately, this stunning formation collapsed into the sea in 2017, but its memory lives on through countless photographs and memories. The nearby Inland Sea and Dwejra Bay remain popular destinations for swimming and diving, with underwater caves and reefs to explore. Gozo's coastline is a tapestry of cliffs, hidden coves, and sandy beaches. Ramla Bay, with its distinctive reddish-gold sand, is a favorite among locals and tourists alike. San Blas Bay, a smaller and more secluded beach, offers a pristine escape for those seeking solitude by the sea.

The island's interior is a patchwork of green fields, rustic villages, and rolling hills. Agriculture is a way of life on Gozo, with farmers tending to vineyards, olive groves, and fields of produce. The fertile soil and favorable climate produce some of Malta's finest fruits and vegetables, including juicy tomatoes and sweet melons.

Gozo's villages, with their charming town squares and historic churches, are a testament to the island's enduring traditions. Victoria, also known as Rabat, serves as Gozo's capital and is home to the imposing Cittadella, a fortified city that has protected Gozitans for centuries.

The island is steeped in history, with archaeological sites dating back to prehistoric times. Ggantija, a Neolithic temple complex, predates the pyramids of Egypt and is a UNESCO World Heritage Site. It offers a fascinating glimpse into the island's ancient past.

Gozo's culture is deeply rooted in music, folklore, and religious traditions. Festivals and celebrations, such as the Festa Ghawdex, bring the island's communities together in vibrant displays of devotion and joy.

With its slower pace of life, Gozo has become a haven for those seeking respite from the hustle and bustle of modern living. Visitors come to hike the scenic trails, explore historic sites, and savor fresh, locally sourced cuisine in family-run restaurants.

In summary, Gozo is Malta's well-kept secret, a sister island that offers a serene and idyllic escape. Its natural beauty, rich history, and traditional way of life combine to create a destination that feels like a journey back in time. For those who seek tranquility, culture, and a connection to the natural world, Gozo is a place where joy can truly be found.

Comino: The Blue Lagoon Paradise

Tucked away between the larger islands of Malta and Gozo lies the tiny but enchanting island of Comino. Although it measures just 3.5 square kilometers (1.4 square miles) in size, Comino's pristine beauty and the legendary Blue Lagoon make it a must-visit destination for those seeking a Mediterranean paradise.

The Blue Lagoon is the crown jewel of Comino, and its name alone conjures images of crystal-clear waters, brilliant azure hues, and endless serenity. This natural wonder is a sheltered inlet nestled between Comino and the uninhabited islet of Cominotto. The lagoon's shallow, transparent waters are so clear that you can see the vibrant marine life swimming below, making it a haven for snorkelers and divers.

One of the lagoon's defining features is its brilliant white sand seabed, which creates a striking contrast to the vibrant blue waters. The combination of colors is simply breathtaking, and it's easy to see why the Blue Lagoon is a top spot for swimming, sunbathing, and relaxation.

Comino itself is a tranquil haven, with a population of just a handful of residents. The island's name is believed to have been derived from the cumin herb, which once grew abundantly here. Beyond the Blue Lagoon, Comino offers visitors the opportunity to explore its rugged terrain, including the towering cliffs that provide a spectacular view of the lagoon from above.

St. Mary's Tower, a 17th-century fortress built by the Knights of St. John, stands as a sentinel on the island. This historic structure served as a defense against pirates and marauders during Malta's turbulent history and is a reminder of Comino's strategic importance.

The island's relatively untouched landscapes make it an ideal destination for nature lovers and hikers. Walking trails crisscross the island, leading you through fields of wildflowers, fragrant herbs, and unique rock formations. Birdwatchers will also find Comino a delight, as the island is home to various migratory and nesting birds.

Comino's isolation and tranquility have made it a haven for those seeking to escape the hustle and bustle of everyday life. There are no cars on the island, adding to its peaceful charm. Visitors can explore the island on foot or rent bicycles to navigate its scenic paths.

To reach Comino, one typically takes a ferry from either Malta or Gozo. The ferry journey itself provides stunning views of the Maltese coastline and the open sea, setting the stage for the natural beauty that awaits on Comino.

In conclusion, Comino's Blue Lagoon is a natural wonder that encapsulates the essence of Mediterranean paradise. The lagoon's crystal-clear waters, pristine beaches, and serene ambiance make it a haven for those seeking relaxation and natural beauty. Comino, with its untouched landscapes and sense of isolation, offers a respite from the modern world and a chance to immerse oneself in the sheer beauty of the Blue Lagoon.

Traditional Maltese Festivals and Celebrations

Malta's rich cultural tapestry is woven with a vibrant array of traditional festivals and celebrations that offer a fascinating glimpse into the heart and soul of the Maltese people. These events, deeply rooted in history and religious devotion, bring communities together in a spirited display of faith, folklore, and festivity.

One of the most renowned and spectacular celebrations on the Maltese calendar is Easter. The week leading up to Easter Sunday is marked by a series of processions, with each town and village putting on its own unique display of devotion. The Good Friday processions are particularly poignant, with statues depicting scenes from the Passion of Christ paraded through the streets, accompanied by solemn hymns and candlelit processions.

Carnival is another cherished Maltese tradition, celebrated with gusto in the days leading up to Lent. The streets come alive with colorful floats, elaborate costumes, and lively music and dancing. Valletta's Grand Harbour is a popular Carnival hotspot, where revelers don masks and costumes and indulge in sweet treats like 'Prinjolata' and 'Kwarezimal.'

Festa season, with its local village feasts, is a highlight of the Maltese summer. Each village celebrates its patron saint with a grand procession, fireworks, and street decorations. The air is filled with the scent of traditional Maltese food, including 'qubbajt' (nougat) and 'ftira biz-zejt' (a delicious bread with tomatoes, capers, and olives). St. Paul's Shipwreck, celebrated on February 10th, is one of Malta's most important religious feasts. It commemorates the shipwreck of the Apostle Paul on the island, an event that plays a significant role in Maltese history and identity. The celebrations include church services, processions, and traditional band marches.

The Feast of Our Lady of the Assumption on August 15th is a national holiday and a major religious celebration. It honors the Assumption of the Virgin Mary and is marked by processions, church services, and the colorful regatta in the Grand Harbour.

The Feast of St. George, celebrated in Qormi, is known for its horse races and traditional 'festa' food. The highlight is the colorful procession of St. George on horseback, symbolizing the victory of good over evil.

Cultural events like the Malta International Fireworks Festival, held in April, and the Valletta International Baroque Festival, held in January, draw artists and spectators from around the world. These festivals showcase Malta's cultural diversity and artistic talent.

Traditional music and dance are integral to Maltese celebrations. The 'għana' is a unique form of folk music that combines poetry, storytelling, and emotional expression. Folk dancers, known as 'il-ħlejjeġ,' perform lively dances at festivals and events.

In conclusion, the traditional festivals and celebrations of Malta offer a window into the island's rich heritage and deep-rooted traditions. These events, whether religious or cultural, are a testament to the Maltese people's passion for their history, faith, and community. They provide an opportunity for visitors to immerse themselves in the vibrant tapestry of Maltese culture, where centuries-old traditions continue to thrive in the modern world.

Maltese Folklore and Superstitions

Malta's rich tapestry of folklore and superstitions is a testament to the island's deep-rooted traditions and the enduring influence of its history, culture, and religion. These beliefs have been passed down through generations, shaping the daily lives and customs of the Maltese people.

One of the most enduring superstitions in Malta revolves around the "evil eye," known as "L-Iharrar." It's believed that envious or malevolent glances from others can bring misfortune, illness, or bad luck. To ward off the evil eye, many Maltese homes feature a small, blue glass ornament called a "ghajn," which is said to absorb the negative energy.

Another fascinating belief is in the "kenniesa," a legendary Maltese witch. It's said that the kenniesa can cast spells and curses, and her name is often whispered in hushed tones. To protect against her malevolent powers, some Maltese households place a broomstick near the entrance, with the bristles facing outwards to sweep away any negative energy.

The "Stregone" is another figure in Maltese folklore, known for practicing dark magic. He is believed to be a shapeshifter who can take on the form of animals or birds. To ward off the Stregone's curses, some Maltese would place a bowl of salt and water under their beds.

Intriguingly, Maltese fishermen have a unique superstition involving bananas. It's considered bad luck to have bananas on board a fishing boat, and many believe that the presence of this fruit will lead to a poor catch. This superstition likely has nautical origins, with seafarers avoiding bananas because they tend to ripen quickly and attract insects, potentially causing problems during long sea journeys. Many traditional Maltese homes feature a "kantuniera," a small shrine or niche typically dedicated to a patron saint. These kantunieras are often adorned with religious statues and candles, serving as a focal point for prayer and veneration. They are believed to protect the home and its inhabitants from harm.

The Feast of St. Anthony's Bread, celebrated on June 13th, is deeply rooted in Maltese tradition. It involves the baking of special loaves of bread, known as "qagħaq tal-appostli," which are distributed to the poor and those in need. It's believed that these breads carry blessings and can bring prosperity.

During the Feast of St. Paul's Shipwreck, celebrated on February 10th, it's customary to consume a traditional Maltese dessert known as "mqaret." These pastries are made with a sweet filling of dates, mixed with flavors like aniseed and orange blossom water, wrapped in thin pastry, and deep-fried to golden perfection.

Maltese wedding customs are steeped in symbolism and superstition. For example, the groom often pins a small iron cross to his jacket to ward off evil spirits. The bride's bouquet typically includes a sprig of rosemary, symbolizing love and remembrance, and a silver sixpence for prosperity.

In conclusion, Maltese folklore and superstitions are an integral part of the island's culture and heritage. These beliefs, ranging from the protective charms against the evil eye to the intriguing legends of witches and shapeshifters, offer a fascinating glimpse into the mindset and traditions of the Maltese people. They are a testament to the enduring influence of history, faith, and community in shaping the unique identity of Malta.

Art and Architecture in Malta

Malta's art and architecture tell a story that spans millennia, reflecting the island's rich history and the influences of various civilizations that have left their mark. From ancient temples to grand Baroque churches and modern galleries, Malta's artistic and architectural heritage is a testament to its enduring cultural significance.

One of the most iconic architectural marvels in Malta is the Megalithic Temples, a UNESCO World Heritage Site. These prehistoric structures, which date back over 5,000 years, are among the oldest free-standing stone buildings in the world. The Ħaġar Qim and Mnajdra Temples, located on the southern coast of Malta, are prime examples of Neolithic architecture and demonstrate the island's deep historical roots.

The Phoenicians, who settled in Malta around 700 BC, left their mark on the island's architecture. Their influence can be seen in the use of sandstone and the distinctive style of megalithic tombs. The most famous of these tombs is the Ħal Saflieni Hypogeum, an underground burial complex that features intricate carvings and chambers, showcasing the advanced skills of the ancient inhabitants.

When the Romans conquered Malta in 218 BC, they brought with them architectural elements that would influence Malta's building style for centuries. Roman villas, bathhouses, and catacombs are scattered across the island, offering a glimpse into daily life during that era.

The arrival of Christianity in the 4th century AD marked a significant turning point in Malta's architecture. Early Christian catacombs, such as the St. Paul's Catacombs in Rabat, are evidence of the island's conversion to Christianity. These underground burial sites are adorned with frescoes and intricate carvings.

The Arab and Byzantine periods in Malta's history also left their architectural imprint. The Arab influence can be seen in the use of arches, while Byzantine mosaics adorned churches and basilicas.

The Knights of St. John, who ruled Malta from 1530 to 1798, are perhaps the most influential in shaping Malta's architectural landscape. They built fortifications such as Fort St. Elmo and the impressive city of Valletta, which is a UNESCO World Heritage Site. Valletta's architecture is a prime example of Baroque and Renaissance styles, with grand palaces, churches, and squares adorned with intricate facades and sculptures.

The Church of St. John in Valletta, known for its opulent interior and Caravaggio's masterpiece, "The Beheading of Saint John the Baptist," is a testament to the artistic prowess of the Knights. Their influence extended to the construction of Auberges (lodges) for the various Langues (nationalities) of the Order, each showcasing unique architectural features.

The 19th and 20th centuries brought architectural diversity to Malta. British rule introduced elements of Victorian and Neo-Gothic architecture, which can be seen in structures like the Anglican Cathedral in Valletta. Art Nouveau and Art Deco styles also found their place in the island's architecture during this period.

Today, Malta's contemporary architecture embraces both tradition and innovation. Modern buildings, such as the Parliament House in Valletta and the City Gate project, blend seamlessly with the historic surroundings while incorporating sustainable design principles.

The Maltese art scene is equally vibrant, with numerous galleries and museums showcasing the works of local and international artists. The National Museum of Fine Arts in Valletta houses an extensive collection of Maltese art, while institutions like the Malta Contemporary Art and the Valletta Contemporary bring contemporary art to the forefront.

In summary, Malta's art and architecture are a testament to the island's rich and diverse history. From ancient temples to grand Baroque churches, the influence of various civilizations and periods has shaped Malta's cultural identity. Today, modern architecture and contemporary art coexist harmoniously with these historic treasures, making Malta a unique and captivating destination for art and architecture enthusiasts.

Music and Dance: A Cultural Melting Pot

Malta's vibrant music and dance traditions reflect the island's rich history as a crossroads of civilizations. This cultural melting pot has given birth to a unique and diverse musical heritage that continues to thrive, captivating both locals and visitors alike.

One of the most distinctive forms of traditional Maltese music is known as "għana." Rooted in folk traditions, għana is a lyrical art form that combines poetry, storytelling, and emotional expression. Typically performed by a solo singer, or "għannej," accompanied by a guitar or lute, għana delves into themes of love, politics, and daily life. The intricate rhyming patterns and improvisational style make each performance a captivating and unique experience.

The "kantilena" is another traditional Maltese song form, characterized by its melodic simplicity and storytelling nature. Kantilena songs have been sung for generations and often convey tales of heroism and love.

During the Baroque period, Malta experienced a surge in musical activity, primarily driven by the influence of the Knights of St. John. These noble knights, hailing from different European regions, brought with them their own musical traditions, enriching Malta's cultural landscape. The city of Valletta, a UNESCO World Heritage Site, became a hub of musical creativity, with grand churches and palaces hosting performances by renowned composers and musicians.

Malta's sacred music tradition is particularly notable, with numerous churches featuring stunning choirs and organs. The annual Good Friday processions are accompanied by hauntingly beautiful choral music that adds a profound emotional depth to the religious ceremonies.

Folk music and dance are integral to Maltese celebrations and festivals. Traditional instruments like the "żaqq," a type of bagpipe, and the "tanbur," a stringed instrument, feature prominently in folk music ensembles. Folk dances like the "għana tar-rummien" and the "fjakkolata" are often performed during village feasts and other celebrations, with lively footwork and spirited rhythms.

The influence of neighboring countries is evident in Maltese music and dance. Italian and Sicilian traditions have left their mark, particularly in the use of instruments like the accordion and the mandolin. Maltese folk music also shares similarities with the music of North Africa and the Middle East, reflecting the island's geographic location and historical ties.

In recent years, Malta's music scene has embraced modern genres, including pop, rock, and electronic music. Local artists have gained international recognition, and music festivals like the Isle of MTV Malta draw thousands of music enthusiasts from around the world.

Dance is another integral part of Malta's cultural fabric. Traditional Maltese dance includes the "bajtar tax-xewk," a lively grape-picking dance, and the "dghajsa" dance, inspired by the rowing of the traditional Maltese boat.

These dances are often performed at festivals and events, keeping the island's heritage alive.

In conclusion, Malta's music and dance traditions are a testament to the island's rich and diverse cultural heritage. From the ancient art of għana to the influence of the Baroque era and the fusion of modern genres, Malta's music continues to evolve while preserving its deep-rooted traditions. Whether it's the emotive storytelling of għana, the lively footwork of folk dances, or the contemporary beats of local musicians, Malta's music and dance scene offer a captivating glimpse into the island's cultural soul.

Maltese Crafts and Artisans

The island of Malta has a rich tradition of craftsmanship that spans centuries, reflecting the island's history, culture, and natural resources. Maltese artisans have honed their skills and passed down their crafts through generations, creating an array of handmade products that are both functional and works of art.

One of the most iconic crafts associated with Malta is the intricate art of filigree. Filigree is the delicate process of weaving fine threads of gold or silver into intricate patterns to create jewelry, often adorned with semi-precious stones. Maltese filigree is renowned for its precision and beauty, and skilled artisans continue to produce stunning pieces that are treasured as heirlooms.

Lace-making is another revered craft in Malta. Maltese lace, particularly the delicate "Maltese Cross" design, is a testament to the patience and skill of the island's lace-makers. Lace-making is often passed down through generations, with artisans meticulously crafting tablecloths, doilies, and other intricate lace pieces that are highly sought after by collectors and tourists.

The craft of glassblowing has a strong presence in Malta, particularly on the neighboring island of Gozo. Skilled glassblowers transform molten glass into a dazzling array of colorful and artistic glassware, including vases, ornaments, and jewelry. The glassblowing tradition in Malta dates back to the Phoenician period, and artisans today continue to blend traditional techniques with contemporary designs.

Pottery is yet another craft deeply rooted in Maltese culture. The island's distinctive terracotta pottery is known for its durability and rustic charm. Artisans craft a variety of functional and decorative pieces, including bowls, plates, and decorative tiles, often adorned with traditional Maltese designs.

The Maltese cross, a symbol of the Knights of St. John, features prominently in Maltese craftsmanship. It can be found adorning a wide range of handmade items, from jewelry to woodwork and textiles. The Maltese cross serves as a symbol of pride and heritage for the island's artisans.

Woodworking and carpentry are essential crafts in Malta, with artisans creating furniture, doors, and intricate wooden designs for homes and churches. These craftsmen skillfully carve and shape wood into exquisite pieces that blend functionality with artistic expression.

The island's history as a maritime nation has also given rise to boat-building as a significant craft. Traditional Maltese fishing boats, known as "luzzu," are handcrafted by skilled artisans. These colorful boats, adorned with the iconic "Eye of Osiris" for protection, are not only functional but also serve as a symbol of Malta's seafaring heritage.

Basket weaving is another time-honored craft, with artisans using natural materials like palm leaves and reeds to create baskets of various shapes and sizes. These baskets are not only practical for everyday use but are also popular souvenirs for visitors.

Malta's crafts and artisans continue to thrive in the modern era, with many workshops and studios welcoming visitors to witness the creative process firsthand. The appreciation for handmade, locally crafted products is strong among both locals and tourists, ensuring that these traditional crafts remain an integral part of Malta's cultural identity.

In conclusion, Maltese crafts and artisans are the custodians of a rich cultural heritage that reflects the island's history and traditions. From the delicate art of filigree to the rustic beauty of pottery, these crafts continue to flourish, providing both functional items and artistic treasures that celebrate Malta's unique identity. The dedication and skill of Maltese artisans ensure that these crafts remain a vibrant and enduring part of the island's cultural tapestry.

The Maltese Language and Its Unique Features

The Maltese language, often referred to as "Maltese" or "Il-Lingwa Maltija," is a fascinating linguistic gem with a history as rich and diverse as the culture of the Maltese Islands themselves. It is the only official Semitic language written in the Latin script, making it a truly unique linguistic blend that reflects the complex history and influences that have shaped Malta.

At its core, Maltese is a Semitic language with deep-rooted connections to Arabic. The earliest form of the language, known as "Siculo-Arabic," emerged during the Arab rule of Malta, which lasted from the 9th to the 13th century. This period of Arab influence significantly impacted the linguistic landscape of the island, leaving a lasting imprint on Maltese vocabulary, phonetics, and grammar.

One of the most distinctive features of Maltese is its Semitic vocabulary, particularly the prevalence of Arabic words. Approximately 40% of the Maltese lexicon is of Arabic origin, and these words encompass a wide range of everyday topics, from family and food to religion and nature. This linguistic legacy serves as a testament to Malta's historical ties to the Arab world.

Despite its Arabic influence, Maltese is not mutually intelligible with standard Arabic dialects. Instead, it has evolved into a distinct language with its own grammatical structure and vocabulary. The evolution of Maltese has been shaped by centuries of contact with various European languages, including Italian, Sicilian, and English.

The Latin script used to write Maltese is another notable feature. The Maltese alphabet consists of 30 letters, including the standard Latin characters as well as some additional diacritics, such as "ċ," "għ," "ħ," "j," and "ż." These diacritics are essential for representing unique Maltese phonemes, adding complexity and depth to the language.

Maltese grammar exhibits both Semitic and Romance characteristics. It uses a predominantly Subject-Verb-Object (SVO) word order, like Romance languages such as Italian and Spanish. However, Maltese retains some Semitic features, such as the use of prepositions instead of articles and the placement of the definite article at the end of nouns. For example, "the cat" in Maltese is "il-qaħba," where "il" is the definite article.

The presence of loanwords from Italian and English further enriches the Maltese language. Italian loanwords are particularly prevalent in domains like cuisine, where dishes like "pastizzi" (savory pastries) and "cannoli" (a dessert) have become staples of Maltese culture. English loanwords, on the other hand, have infiltrated modern life, with terms like "computer" and "television" adopted directly from English.

Maltese is also known for its unique pronunciation, characterized by distinctive consonant clusters and guttural sounds. The sounds represented by the letters "ċ," "għ," and "ħ" are among the most challenging for non-native speakers to master. These phonetic nuances give the language its musical and rhythmic quality, making it instantly recognizable to those familiar with it.

In recent years, there has been a concerted effort to preserve and promote the Maltese language, with initiatives aimed at increasing its usage in education, media, and daily life. The Maltese government recognizes the importance of preserving this linguistic heritage, and Maltese is one of the official languages of the European Union.

In conclusion, the Maltese language is a captivating linguistic fusion that reflects the island's rich history, blending Semitic and Romance elements into a unique and distinct linguistic tapestry. Its Arabic influence, Latin script, and distinctive phonetics make it a language that continues to evolve while honoring its historical roots. As a symbol of Maltese identity, the language plays a vital role in preserving the cultural heritage of the Maltese Islands.

Religion in Malta: Faith and Tradition

Religion has long played a central role in the cultural and social fabric of Malta. The Maltese Islands are known for their deep-rooted religious traditions, with the majority of the population adhering to the Roman Catholic faith. This chapter explores the significance of religion in Malta, tracing its history, traditions, and impact on daily life.

The Maltese people have a proud and enduring connection to the Roman Catholic Church, and Catholicism has been the state religion of Malta since 1964. The presence of the Catholic Church in Malta dates back to the early centuries of Christianity, making it one of the oldest Christian communities in the world. The island's religious heritage is celebrated through an array of churches, chapels, and religious festivals that dot the landscape.

The Maltese archipelago boasts an impressive number of churches, many of which are architectural marvels. The most famous of these is St. John's Co-Cathedral in Valletta, renowned for its opulent interior, artistic treasures, and Caravaggio's masterpieces. The Maltese countryside is adorned with charming village churches, each with its own unique character and history.

Religious festivals hold a special place in the hearts of the Maltese people. These celebrations, known as "festi," are dedicated to patron saints and are marked by elaborate processions, colorful decorations, fireworks, and traditional music. The feast of St. Paul's Shipwreck in February and the feast of Our Lady of Victories in September are among the most prominent.

The village of Żebbuġ is famous for its Good Friday procession, a solemn and moving event that draws crowds of both locals and tourists. During the procession, the faithful reenact the Stations of the Cross, portraying scenes from the Passion of Christ.

The religious calendar in Malta is punctuated by various feasts and observances, each with its own unique traditions and rituals. From the Nativity of Our Lady to the feast of the Immaculate Conception, these religious events provide a glimpse into the deep spirituality that permeates Maltese life.

Beyond the Catholic tradition, Malta has a small but diverse religious landscape. The Maltese Constitution guarantees freedom of religion, and there are various religious denominations present, including Anglicans, Muslims, and other Christian denominations. These religious communities coexist peacefully, contributing to Malta's reputation as a harmonious and tolerant society.

The Maltese Islands have also been a destination for religious pilgrimage. The Sanctuary of Our Lady of Mellieħa and the Basilica of Ta' Pinu on the island of Gozo are revered pilgrimage sites for Catholics and draw visitors seeking spiritual solace.

Religion in Malta extends beyond religious practices and rituals; it is woven into the very fabric of daily life. Family gatherings, traditions, and values are often deeply rooted in religious beliefs. Sunday Mass remains a significant cultural and social event, bringing families and communities together.

In recent years, there has been a renewed emphasis on interfaith dialogue and religious tolerance in Malta. The government has actively promoted initiatives to foster understanding and respect among different religious communities, recognizing the importance of religious diversity in the modern world.

In conclusion, religion in Malta is a powerful and enduring force that shapes the identity and culture of the Maltese people. The Catholic faith, with its rich traditions and vibrant celebrations, continues to hold a central place in the hearts of the Maltese. Yet, Malta's religious landscape is also marked by diversity and tolerance, reflecting the island's commitment to inclusivity and harmony. Religion in Malta remains a living testament to the enduring power of faith and tradition in a rapidly changing world.

Education and Healthcare in Malta

Education and healthcare are two cornerstones of a well-functioning society, and in Malta, they are no exception. The Maltese Islands have made significant strides in both these crucial sectors, providing its citizens with access to quality education and healthcare services.

Education in Malta is compulsory for children between the ages of 5 and 16, with a robust educational system in place to ensure that all students receive a well-rounded education. The education system in Malta is bilingual, with Maltese and English as the official languages of instruction. This bilingual approach reflects Malta's historical ties with both the Mediterranean and the British Empire.

The Maltese education system is divided into various stages, including early childhood education, primary education, secondary education, and tertiary education. Primary and secondary education are free and provided by the government, making education accessible to all Maltese citizens. Additionally, there is a strong emphasis on religious education, reflecting the country's Catholic tradition.

Malta's primary and secondary schools have consistently achieved high standards of education, with students generally performing well in international assessments. The Maltese government places great importance on investing in education, and this commitment is evident in the quality of school facilities, resources, and qualified teachers.

For higher education, Malta is home to the University of Malta, the country's only public university. The University of Malta offers a wide range of undergraduate and postgraduate programs, attracting students from both Malta and abroad. The university's academic reputation continues to grow, and it plays a vital role in Malta's efforts to promote research and innovation.

In addition to the University of Malta, there are several private institutions offering specialized courses and programs, contributing to the diversification of educational opportunities on the islands.

Turning to healthcare, Malta has a comprehensive healthcare system that provides accessible and quality medical services to its residents. Healthcare in Malta is funded through a combination of taxation and social security contributions, ensuring that healthcare services are available to all, regardless of their financial status.

Public healthcare in Malta is primarily provided by the Ministry for Health, and the country boasts a network of health centers and hospitals. Mater Dei Hospital, the largest and most advanced hospital in Malta, offers a wide range of medical services and is equipped with state-of-the-art facilities. The quality of healthcare in Malta is generally high, and the country has made significant advancements in medical research and technology.

Malta also has a vibrant private healthcare sector, allowing patients to choose between public and private healthcare providers. This dual system offers a level of flexibility and choice for residents seeking medical care.

Pharmaceutical services are readily available through a network of pharmacies across the islands, ensuring that patients have access to prescription and over-the-counter medications when needed.

Malta's healthcare system places a strong emphasis on preventive medicine, with regular health check-ups and vaccination programs. Additionally, the country has a robust public health infrastructure that responds effectively to public health emergencies and crises.

In conclusion, education and healthcare in Malta are pillars of the nation's commitment to providing a high quality of life for its citizens. The educational system's bilingual approach and the accessibility of healthcare services reflect Malta's dedication to the well-being and development of its people. As Malta continues to evolve and face new challenges, the resilience and adaptability of its education and healthcare systems remain fundamental in ensuring the prosperity and welfare of its population.

Malta's Economy and Industries

Malta, a picturesque archipelago in the heart of the Mediterranean, has experienced significant economic growth and transformation in recent decades. This chapter delves into the multifaceted aspects of Malta's economy, exploring its key industries, trade relationships, and the factors that have contributed to its economic prosperity.

Malta's economy is characterized by its resilience, diversification, and openness to international trade. Over the years, the country has transitioned from a predominantly agrarian society to a modern, service-oriented economy. Today, the services sector plays a pivotal role in Malta's economic landscape, contributing significantly to its Gross Domestic Product (GDP).

One of the driving forces behind Malta's economic success is its status as a European Union (EU) member state. Membership in the EU has granted Malta access to a vast single market and has facilitated trade relationships with other EU countries. The adoption of the euro as its official currency has further integrated Malta into the Eurozone, promoting financial stability and investment.

The financial services sector in Malta has experienced remarkable growth, with the country becoming an attractive destination for international businesses seeking a European presence. The Maltese financial services industry encompasses banking, insurance, asset management, and fintech. The Malta Financial Services Authority (MFSA) oversees the regulatory framework, ensuring compliance with international standards.

Tourism is another pillar of Malta's economy, drawing millions of visitors annually. The island's rich history, cultural heritage, and stunning Mediterranean landscapes make it a sought-after destination. The tourism industry encompasses a wide range of services, from hospitality and leisure to cultural tourism, contributing significantly to employment and GDP.

Manufacturing has historically been a vital sector in Malta's economy, with a focus on pharmaceuticals, electronics, and aerospace. Foreign direct investment (FDI) has played a crucial role in driving industrial development, attracting multinational corporations seeking a strategic European location.

Malta's strategic location in the Mediterranean has made it a hub for maritime activities and logistics. The country's ports and shipping services facilitate international trade and transshipment, connecting Europe with North Africa and the Middle East.

The information technology and gaming industry have also experienced remarkable growth in Malta. The country is home to numerous iGaming companies, attracted by its regulatory framework and skilled workforce. This sector continues to expand, with Malta positioning itself as a hub for digital innovation.

Agriculture, although less prominent than in the past, remains an important part of Malta's economy. The country produces a variety of crops, including tomatoes, potatoes, and citrus fruits, while also engaging in animal husbandry.

Malta's economy is underpinned by a skilled and educated workforce, with an emphasis on vocational training and tertiary education. The labor force is proficient in languages, particularly English, which contributes to its attractiveness as a destination for international business and services.

Despite its small size and limited natural resources, Malta's economic resilience and adaptability have allowed it to weather economic challenges and emerge as a thriving and diversified economy. The government's commitment to innovation, sustainability, and economic development continue to position Malta as an attractive destination for investment and business growth.

In conclusion, Malta's economy is a testament to its ability to evolve and adapt in a changing global landscape. The country's emphasis on services, financial services, tourism, manufacturing, and technology has propelled its economic growth and prosperity. Malta's strategic location, EU membership, and commitment to innovation ensure its continued relevance in the international economic arena.

Transportation and Infrastructure

The efficient movement of people and goods is a fundamental aspect of any thriving society, and Malta is no exception. This chapter explores the transportation and infrastructure landscape of the Maltese Islands, highlighting the key elements that keep this Mediterranean nation connected and accessible.

One of Malta's most notable transportation features is its road network. Despite its small size, Malta boasts a dense network of well-maintained roads that connect various towns and villages. The road system includes highways, arterial roads, and smaller local roads, providing convenient access to different parts of the islands. The adoption of the EuroVelo cycling network has also encouraged cycling as an eco-friendly mode of transportation.

Public transportation in Malta is primarily managed by the Malta Public Transport (MPT) company, which operates an extensive bus network. Buses are a popular means of getting around the islands, offering regular routes that cover urban and rural areas. The introduction of modern, eco-friendly buses has improved the quality of public transportation and encouraged its use.

The road network also plays a crucial role in accommodating private vehicles. Malta has a relatively high rate of car ownership, which is supported by an extensive network of car rental agencies and dealerships. However, traffic congestion can be an issue in urban areas, particularly during rush hours.

In recent years, efforts have been made to encourage sustainable transportation alternatives. Initiatives promoting cycling and the introduction of electric scooters have gained popularity, providing eco-friendly options for commuting and leisure.

Malta's connectivity isn't limited to land-based transportation. The country's international airport, Malta International Airport (MLA), is a vital gateway for travelers. Located in Luqa, the airport is well-connected to major European cities and serves as a significant hub for both tourists and business travelers. MLA's strategic location and modern facilities make it a crucial asset for the Maltese economy.

Maritime transportation is another essential aspect of Malta's connectivity. The country boasts several harbors and ports, including the Grand Harbour in Valletta and the Freeport Terminal in Birżebbuġa. These ports facilitate the import and export of goods, as well as passenger ferry services to neighboring islands and Sicily.

The maritime industry also includes recreational boating and yacht charter services, which capitalize on Malta's stunning coastline and clear waters. The country's harbors are often bustling with activity, attracting both tourists and sailing enthusiasts.

Malta's infrastructure extends beneath the surface with an extensive network of tunnels and underground reservoirs, vital for managing the country's water supply. Due to its limited natural freshwater sources, Malta relies heavily on desalination plants to provide clean drinking water to its residents and visitors.

The energy sector has also seen significant developments in recent years. Malta's electricity generation primarily depends on natural gas and renewable energy sources like solar power and wind energy. The country is actively investing in sustainable energy solutions to reduce its carbon footprint and promote environmental sustainability.

In conclusion, transportation and infrastructure are essential components of Malta's modern and interconnected society. The country's road network, public transportation services, international airport, ports, and maritime industry collectively ensure efficient movement within and beyond the Maltese Islands. Moreover, Malta's commitment to sustainability, from eco-friendly buses to renewable energy sources, reflects its dedication to preserving its natural environment while supporting economic growth and development.

Sports and Leisure Activities in Malta

Malta, with its favorable Mediterranean climate and stunning natural landscapes, offers a diverse range of sports and leisure activities for both residents and visitors to enjoy. From traditional games to modern sporting events, the Maltese Islands cater to a wide spectrum of interests and passions.

Water sports enthusiasts will find Malta to be a paradise. The crystal-clear waters of the Mediterranean are perfect for swimming, snorkeling, scuba diving, and sailing. The islands' numerous diving sites, such as the Blue Hole in Gozo and the Um El Faroud wreck, attract divers from around the world. Malta's underwater world is teeming with marine life, caves, and colorful coral reefs, making it an exceptional destination for underwater exploration.

Sailing is a popular pastime in Malta, with numerous marinas and yacht clubs offering facilities and services for sailors of all levels. The annual Rolex Middle Sea Race, which starts and finishes in Malta, is a prestigious international sailing event that attracts competitive sailors.

For those who prefer land-based activities, hiking and trekking in Malta's countryside are highly rewarding experiences. The islands are crisscrossed with well-marked trails that lead to picturesque landscapes, hidden coves, and historical sites. The Dingli Cliffs, the Victoria Lines, and the various nature reserves provide opportunities for breathtaking hikes and walks.

Cycling is also gaining popularity, thanks to the construction of dedicated cycling lanes and scenic routes. Biking enthusiasts can explore the islands' charming villages, historic sites, and coastal vistas on two wheels.

Football, or soccer, holds a special place in the hearts of the Maltese people. The country boasts a national football league, and matches are a significant part of the sporting calendar. The national team competes in international competitions, showcasing Malta's dedication to the sport.

Horse racing is another sport that has a dedicated following in Malta. The Marsa Race Track hosts regular horse racing events, attracting both locals and tourists looking to enjoy a day at the races.

Malta also offers opportunities for golfers, with a few golf courses available for enthusiasts to practice their swings while taking in scenic views.

Traditional Maltese sports and games, such as bocci and kites, are still enjoyed by local communities. These activities provide a glimpse into Malta's cultural heritage and can often be witnessed during local festivals and events.

Malta's rich history and heritage offer unique opportunities for cultural and historical exploration. The islands are home to numerous museums, archaeological sites, and historical buildings that provide a window into Malta's past. The prehistoric temples of Ħaġar Qim and Mnajdra, the medieval city of Mdina, and the awe-inspiring St. John's Co-Cathedral in Valletta are just a few examples of the historical treasures that await visitors.

In the realm of leisure, Malta's vibrant nightlife is a major draw. The island's bars, clubs, and entertainment venues come alive after sunset, offering a diverse range of experiences for night owls and partygoers.

In conclusion, Malta's sports and leisure offerings cater to a wide range of interests, making it a versatile destination for travelers seeking both active and cultural experiences. Whether it's diving into the Mediterranean's depths, exploring ancient temples, or enjoying the vibrant nightlife, Malta has something for everyone to savor and savor again.

Sustainable Tourism in Malta

In recent years, the concept of sustainable tourism has gained momentum around the world, and Malta has been at the forefront of embracing this approach to preserve its natural beauty and cultural heritage while still catering to the needs of tourists. Sustainable tourism in Malta is not just a buzzword; it's a commitment to preserving the islands' unique ecosystems, minimizing environmental impact, and supporting local communities.

One of the key elements of sustainable tourism in Malta is the protection of its pristine natural environment. The Maltese Islands are home to several Natura 2000 sites, which are designated areas of conservation importance. These sites encompass a variety of habitats, including coastal areas, cliffs, and wetlands, and they are crucial for the protection of Malta's biodiversity.

Efforts have been made to promote responsible behavior among tourists, such as respecting protected areas, not disturbing wildlife, and following established hiking trails. The Maltese government and various environmental organizations are actively involved in conservation initiatives aimed at safeguarding the islands' natural beauty.

The islands are also working toward energy efficiency and renewable energy sources to reduce their carbon footprint. Malta has invested in solar power and wind energy, and energy-saving initiatives have been implemented in hotels and other accommodations.

Water conservation is another essential aspect of sustainable tourism in Malta. The islands have limited freshwater resources, and desalination plants provide much of the drinking water. Tourists are encouraged to use water wisely, and hotels often have water-saving measures in place.

The promotion of local culture and heritage is central to sustainable tourism in Malta. Traditional Maltese crafts, music, and cuisine are celebrated and supported, helping to sustain local communities and preserve cultural traditions. Visitors can enjoy local markets, artisan shops, and traditional festivals that showcase Malta's rich heritage.

Accommodations in Malta increasingly focus on sustainability. Many hotels and guesthouses have implemented eco-friendly practices, from reducing plastic waste to using energy-efficient appliances. Additionally, some accommodations offer eco-certifications to demonstrate their commitment to sustainability.

The Maltese Islands also emphasize responsible tourism activities, such as diving and snorkeling. Tour operators and dive centers adhere to guidelines to protect marine ecosystems and prevent damage to underwater environments.

Education and awareness play a vital role in sustainable tourism in Malta. Tourists are encouraged to learn about the local environment and culture, respect the islands' natural beauty, and support responsible businesses. Information centers and eco-tourism initiatives provide resources to help tourists make informed choices.

Overall, sustainable tourism in Malta is not just a concept; it's a way of life. The islands recognize the importance of balancing tourism with environmental conservation and cultural preservation. By embracing sustainable practices and promoting responsible tourism, Malta ensures that future generations can continue to enjoy the islands' unparalleled beauty and rich heritage.

Exploring Malta's Underwater World

Beneath the azure Mediterranean waters that surround the Maltese Islands lies a hidden world of breathtaking beauty and marine biodiversity. Exploring Malta's underwater world is a captivating adventure that attracts divers and snorkelers from across the globe. With its clear waters, diverse marine life, and a wealth of underwater attractions, Malta is a diver's paradise.

One of the defining features of Malta's underwater realm is its crystal-clear visibility. The waters surrounding the islands are known for their exceptional clarity, often providing visibility of up to 30 meters (98 feet) or more. This pristine visibility allows divers to fully appreciate the stunning underwater landscapes and vibrant marine life.

Malta's coastline is dotted with a myriad of dive sites, each offering a unique underwater experience. From shallow reefs to dramatic drop-offs, underwater caves, and historic wrecks, there is something for divers of all skill levels and interests.

One of the most iconic dive sites in Malta is the Blue Hole in Gozo. This natural sinkhole leads to a breathtaking underwater arch and tunnel system, creating a mesmerizing underwater playground for divers. The Azure Window, a natural limestone arch that stood nearby, unfortunately collapsed in 2017, but the Blue Hole remains a top attraction.

The Um El Faroud wreck is another famous dive site, a 10,000-ton Libyan oil tanker that was scuttled off the coast of Malta to create an artificial reef. This massive wreck has become a haven for marine life and a fascinating exploration for experienced divers.

Malta's underwater world is teeming with marine biodiversity. Divers can encounter colorful fish species, including damselfish, parrotfish, and groupers, as well as a variety of crustaceans and mollusks. The Mediterranean Sea is also home to unique species like seahorses and the charismatic Mediterranean moray eel.

For those interested in underwater photography, Malta provides excellent opportunities to capture the beauty of the marine world. The play of sunlight on the seabed, the intricate details of marine life, and the dramatic underwater landscapes make for stunning photographic subjects.

The islands' underwater caves are another intriguing aspect of Malta's diving experience. These submerged caverns and tunnels offer a sense of exploration and adventure, and some even contain ancient artifacts and relics.

Safety and conservation are top priorities for Malta's diving community. Dive centers and instructors adhere to strict safety protocols, and marine conservation efforts are ongoing. Divers are encouraged to respect the delicate marine environment, avoid touching or disturbing marine life, and follow responsible diving practices.

Snorkeling is also a popular activity in Malta, offering a more accessible way to explore the underwater world. Many of the shallow reefs and coves can be explored with just a mask, snorkel, and fins, making it an ideal activity for families and beginners.

In conclusion, exploring Malta's underwater world is a journey into a realm of wonder and discovery. With its exceptional visibility, diverse marine life, and captivating dive sites, Malta offers an unparalleled underwater experience for divers and snorkelers alike. Whether you're an experienced diver seeking adventure or a novice snorkeler looking to connect with nature, Malta's marine world invites you to dive in and explore its secrets.

A Glimpse into Malta's Film Industry

Nestled in the heart of the Mediterranean, the Maltese Islands have served as a backdrop for numerous film productions, earning their place on the global stage of the film industry. Malta's diverse landscapes, historic sites, and skilled workforce have attracted filmmakers from around the world, contributing to the country's emerging prominence in the cinematic realm.

One of the defining characteristics of Malta's film industry is its versatility in doubling for various locations. The islands' landscapes can seamlessly transform into ancient cities, mythical realms, or futuristic dystopias. This chameleon-like quality has made Malta an attractive destination for filmmakers seeking diverse settings for their stories.

Historical epics have often found their home in Malta. Productions like "Gladiator" (2000) and "Troy" (2004) utilized Malta's ancient fortifications and architectural treasures to recreate ancient civilizations. The medieval walled city of Mdina, with its narrow streets and centuries-old buildings, has been a favored location for historical dramas.

Malta's connection to Hollywood was solidified when Steven Spielberg chose the island as the backdrop for "Munich" (2005), a gripping thriller that recounts the aftermath of the 1972 Munich Olympics massacre. Spielberg's decision to film in Malta showcased the country's growing reputation in the film industry.

The islands' natural beauty has also attracted filmmakers. The stunning cliffs and crystal-clear waters have served as settings for various action sequences and aquatic scenes. The iconic Azure Window, a natural limestone arch on the island of Gozo, famously featured in "Game of Thrones."

In addition to its landscapes, Malta boasts modern film facilities and a skilled workforce. The Mediterranean Film Studios, located in Kalkara, provide state-of-the-art facilities for filmmakers, including underwater tanks and green screens. The local film industry has nurtured a pool of talented professionals, from actors and directors to cinematographers and set designers.

The Malta Film Commission plays a pivotal role in supporting and promoting the country's film industry. It offers incentives, rebates, and logistical support to attract international productions. These efforts have resulted in collaborations with major studios and filmmakers worldwide.

Malta has also hosted a range of international film festivals, further solidifying its presence in the global film community. The Valletta Film Festival, for instance, showcases a diverse selection of international films and provides a platform for local talent.

Malta's emerging film industry not only contributes to its economy but also enriches its cultural landscape. Local filmmakers are increasingly producing films that explore Malta's history, culture, and contemporary society, gaining recognition both at home and abroad.

In conclusion, Malta's film industry is a testament to the country's ability to captivate and inspire filmmakers worldwide. Its diverse landscapes, historical treasures, modern facilities, and supportive infrastructure have positioned Malta as a versatile and sought-after destination for filmmakers. As the country continues to evolve as a cinematic hub, it opens doors for both local and international talent to tell their stories against the backdrop of this Mediterranean gem.

Malta's Role in World War II

Malta, a tiny Mediterranean archipelago, found itself in the midst of one of the most significant conflicts in history during World War II. Its strategic location made it a crucial battleground, and its resilience and determination earned it the title of "The Most Bombed Place on Earth." Malta's role in World War II was defined by its steadfast defense, unwavering spirit, and its ability to withstand relentless enemy attacks.

At the outbreak of World War II in 1939, Malta was a British colony. Its strategic importance became immediately apparent to both the Axis and Allied powers. Situated in the central Mediterranean, Malta was a vital link for controlling shipping routes and air access in the region. Possessing Malta meant controlling the flow of supplies and reinforcements to North Africa, which was a critical theater of the war.

The Axis powers, particularly Germany and Italy, recognized the significance of Malta and began a relentless campaign to neutralize the island. They subjected Malta to a continuous aerial bombardment, with the goal of rendering its ports and airfields unusable and starving the island into submission.

Malta's defenses were led by a determined group of British and Maltese military personnel. The island was heavily fortified, with coastal guns, anti-aircraft batteries, and underground tunnels. The Royal Air Force (RAF) and Royal Navy played pivotal roles in defending the island against air raids and naval attacks.

The Maltese population endured unimaginable hardships during this period. The island was subjected to near-constant bombardment, leading to severe food and fuel shortages. The citizens of Malta displayed immense resilience, withstanding the relentless attacks and contributing to the defense effort. King George VI awarded the George Cross to the island in 1942 in recognition of the population's bravery and fortitude.

The Siege of Malta, as it came to be known, was a protracted and grueling battle. The island's defenders faced not only aerial bombardment but also naval blockades and submarine attacks. Yet, Malta's strategic importance meant that the Allies were determined to keep it in their hands.

The arrival of relief convoys, often under heavy escort, brought essential supplies to Malta. These convoys faced fierce opposition from Axis forces but played a crucial role in ensuring the island's survival.

One of the most iconic episodes of Malta's wartime history was the involvement of the British aircraft carrier HMS Ark Royal. Its aircraft, particularly the Swordfish torpedo bombers, played a pivotal role in sinking the Italian battleships Littorio and Conte di Cavour, severely hampering the Axis naval blockade.

Malta's strategic significance increased as the Allies launched the North African Campaign. The island became a base for air raids and submarine operations against Axis supply lines to North Africa.

By the time World War II ended in 1945, Malta had endured 1,500 bombing raids and countless other attacks. The island's people had suffered greatly, but their resilience had paid off. Malta's role in World War II was crucial in securing the Mediterranean and North African theaters for the Allies.

Today, Malta's wartime history is remembered and commemorated. The island's capital, Valletta, was awarded the title of a UNESCO World Heritage Site in recognition of its historic significance during the war. The Malta War Museum and various other sites and memorials serve as reminders of the sacrifices made by the Maltese people and their role in a global conflict that forever shaped the course of history.

Malta's Political Landscape

Malta, a small island nation in the Mediterranean, boasts a rich and dynamic political landscape that reflects its complex history, vibrant culture, and diverse population. Understanding Malta's political landscape requires delving into its historical roots, its constitutional framework, and the contemporary political forces that shape its governance.

Historically, Malta has been at the crossroads of various civilizations, including the Phoenicians, Romans, Arabs, Knights of St. John, French, and British. Each of these influences has left an indelible mark on the country's political, social, and cultural development. Malta's strategic location in the Mediterranean has made it a coveted prize for numerous empires throughout history.

One of the most significant turning points in Malta's political history occurred in 1964 when it gained independence from British colonial rule. The country became a constitutional monarchy within the British Commonwealth, with Queen Elizabeth II as its head of state. However, this status was short-lived, as Malta transitioned to a republic in 1974, with its first president, Sir Anthony Mamo.

Malta's political system is parliamentary democracy, and its political landscape is characterized by a multi-party system. The two dominant political parties are the Labour Party (Partit Laburista) and the Nationalist Party (Partit Nazzjonalista). These parties have historically alternated in power, contributing to a competitive and lively political scene.

The Labour Party, founded in 1921, is a center-left party that advocates for progressive policies, workers' rights, and social justice. It has been in power for significant periods, implementing policies such as healthcare reforms, pension schemes, and educational improvements.

On the other hand, the Nationalist Party, founded in 1880, is a center-right party that champions economic liberalism, privatization, and conservative values. It has also held power and implemented policies that promote economic growth and stability.

Malta's political landscape often sees closely contested elections, reflecting the polarized nature of its politics. This competitive environment has led to a system where both major parties must adapt to the changing needs and aspirations of the electorate.

The Maltese parliament, known as the House of Representatives (Il-Kamra tad-Deputati), consists of 65 members who are elected by proportional representation. The party or coalition that secures the majority in parliament forms the government, and its leader becomes the Prime Minister. The President of Malta, elected by the parliament, serves as the ceremonial head of state.

The political discourse in Malta is not limited to domestic affairs. The country actively participates in international politics and is a member of the United Nations, the European Union, and the Commonwealth of Nations. Malta's foreign policy is shaped by its commitment to peace, diplomacy, and international cooperation.

Malta's political landscape also grapples with contemporary issues such as immigration, environmental sustainability, and economic diversification. As a small nation with a limited landmass and resources, Malta faces unique challenges in managing its population growth, preserving its natural beauty, and ensuring economic sustainability.

In recent years, issues related to good governance and corruption have also come to the forefront of Malta's political discourse, prompting demands for transparency and accountability.

In conclusion, Malta's political landscape is a reflection of its historical legacy, democratic principles, and the aspirations of its people. With a competitive multi-party system, a commitment to democratic values, and active participation on the international stage, Malta continues to evolve and adapt to the changing political dynamics of the 21st century.

Contemporary Issues and Challenges

As Malta navigates the complexities of the 21st century, it faces a set of contemporary issues and challenges that demand careful consideration and innovative solutions. These challenges span various aspects of society, economy, and governance, reflecting the interconnected nature of Malta's place in the global community.

1. **Immigration and Asylum:** One of the most pressing contemporary issues in Malta is the management of immigration and asylum seekers. As a geographically strategic location in the Mediterranean, Malta often serves as a first point of entry for migrants attempting to reach Europe. This challenge includes addressing humanitarian concerns, providing adequate facilities, and addressing the socio-economic integration of newcomers.

2. **Environmental Sustainability:** Malta's limited land area and fragile ecosystem make environmental sustainability a critical concern. Urbanization, overdevelopment, and pressure on natural resources raise questions about the long-term ecological health of the islands. Initiatives to promote renewable energy, protect biodiversity, and address waste management are crucial.

3. **Infrastructure and Congestion:** The rapid growth of Malta's population, combined with tourism, has put significant strain on infrastructure, leading to issues such as traffic congestion, strained public transport, and inadequate road networks. Finding solutions to improve mobility while preserving

Malta's unique cultural and historical heritage is a key challenge.

4. **Economic Diversification:** Historically reliant on sectors like tourism and manufacturing, Malta is working to diversify its economy. Encouraging innovation, nurturing the tech sector, and promoting entrepreneurship are vital to achieving economic stability and resilience.

5. **Good Governance and Corruption:** Ensuring transparency and accountability in government has become increasingly important. Recent scandals and allegations of corruption have raised concerns about the integrity of Malta's institutions. The drive for good governance and anti-corruption measures is a priority.

6. **Social Welfare and Inequality:** Despite economic growth, Malta faces challenges related to income inequality and social welfare. Ensuring that the benefits of economic prosperity are distributed equitably is a concern shared by policymakers and civil society.

7. **Aging Population:** Like many Western nations, Malta is experiencing an aging population. This demographic shift brings challenges related to healthcare, pensions, and the need for a more diverse and adaptable workforce.

8. **Education and Skills:** Preparing the workforce for the demands of a modern economy is a key challenge. This includes enhancing the education system, fostering lifelong learning, and aligning skills with emerging industries.

9. **Cultural Preservation:** Balancing the preservation of Malta's rich cultural heritage with the demands of modernization is a delicate task. Maintaining

historical sites, traditions, and language while embracing progress is a continuing challenge.

10. **Tourism Sustainability:** Tourism, while essential to Malta's economy, must be managed sustainably. Striking a balance between attracting tourists and preserving the environment and local culture is crucial.

11. **Healthcare Infrastructure:** Ensuring accessible, quality healthcare for the population is an ongoing concern, especially given the demands placed on the healthcare system during the COVID-19 pandemic.

12. **Global Connectivity:** As a small island nation, Malta relies heavily on international trade and connectivity. Ensuring robust global connections while navigating changing international dynamics is a contemporary challenge.

Malta's ability to address these contemporary issues and challenges is a testament to its adaptability and resilience. The government, civil society, and the people of Malta are actively engaged in finding innovative solutions and shaping the future of this Mediterranean nation. In an ever-changing world, Malta's ability to adapt while preserving its unique identity will continue to define its success in the 21st century.

Maltese Hospitality and Etiquette

Malta, with its warm Mediterranean climate and rich cultural heritage, is known for its exceptional hospitality and unique etiquette customs. Understanding the social norms and traditions of this island nation is key to fully experiencing the warmth and charm of its people.

1. **Warm Greetings:** Maltese people are known for their warm and friendly nature. It is customary to exchange greetings with a smile and a friendly "hello" or "good morning" when meeting someone, even if it's a stranger. Handshakes are common in more formal settings.

2. **Personal Space:** While Maltese people are friendly, they also value personal space. It's important to maintain a comfortable distance when engaging in conversations or interactions, especially with people you've just met.

3. **Dress Code:** Malta's warm climate often calls for casual attire, but when visiting churches or attending formal events, modest clothing is appreciated. It's customary to cover your shoulders and knees when entering churches out of respect.

4. **Gift-Giving:** When invited to someone's home, bringing a small gift like a bottle of wine, chocolates, or flowers is a thoughtful gesture. Gifts are typically opened when received, and it's polite to express gratitude.

5. **Dining Etiquette:** Maltese cuisine is a delightful mix of Mediterranean flavors, and sharing meals is a common social activity. When dining in a Maltese home or restaurant, it's polite to wait until the host

initiates the meal. Table manners are generally informal, but it's courteous to say "Bon Appétit" before eating.

6. **Language:** While English and Maltese are both official languages, English is widely spoken and understood, making communication easy for visitors. Learning a few Maltese phrases, such as "Bongu" (Good morning) or "Grazzi" (Thank you), is appreciated.

7. **Tipping:** Tipping in Malta is customary but not obligatory. In restaurants, leaving a 10% to 15% tip is appreciated. Tipping is also common in taxis and for other services.

8. **Religious Respect:** Malta is a predominantly Catholic country, and religious traditions are deeply ingrained. Visitors should be respectful when visiting churches, cathedrals, and religious sites, dressing modestly and refraining from loud conversations.

9. **Punctuality:** Maltese people generally value punctuality, so it's courteous to arrive on time for appointments and social gatherings.

10. **Festivals and Celebrations:** Malta hosts a variety of lively festivals and celebrations throughout the year. It's a wonderful opportunity to experience local culture and traditions. Joining in the festivities, whether it's a religious procession or a village feast, is a great way to immerse yourself in Maltese life.

11. **Sundays and Siesta:** Traditionally, Sundays were a day for family gatherings, and many businesses closed. While this is changing in urban areas, Sundays still have a relaxed pace. Additionally, it's worth noting that the siesta tradition is observed in

some areas, with a break in the afternoon for rest and relaxation.

12. **Island Time:** The concept of "island time" is prevalent in Malta. Life tends to move at a more relaxed pace, and it's advisable for visitors to embrace this aspect of Maltese culture and not be in a hurry.

13. **Hospitality:** Maltese people take pride in their hospitality and are known for their generosity. It's common to be offered refreshments when visiting someone's home, and it's polite to accept.

Malta's unique blend of Mediterranean charm and cultural heritage is reflected in its customs and etiquette. Embracing these traditions and showing respect for the local way of life will enhance your experience and allow you to forge meaningful connections with the people of this enchanting island.

Investing and Living in Malta

Malta, with its stunning landscapes, rich history, and thriving economy, has become an attractive destination for both investors and expatriates seeking a unique Mediterranean lifestyle. This chapter explores the opportunities and considerations for those interested in investing and living in Malta.

Economic Landscape: Malta's economy has experienced significant growth in recent years, driven by sectors such as financial services, iGaming, and technology. The country's strategic location and favorable tax incentives have attracted multinational corporations and startups alike. Additionally, Malta is part of the Eurozone, providing stability for investors and businesses.

Residency and Citizenship: Malta offers several residency and citizenship programs for foreign investors. The Malta Individual Investor Program (IIP) and the Malta Residence and Visa Program (MRVP) provide pathways to residency and citizenship, respectively, in exchange for specific investments in the country.

Real Estate Investment: Investing in Maltese real estate is a popular choice for both residents and non-residents. The property market offers a range of options, from historic townhouses in Valletta to modern apartments along the coast. Property prices have been steadily increasing, making real estate an attractive investment.

Business Opportunities: Malta's business-friendly environment encourages entrepreneurship and investment.

The Malta Business Registry streamlines company registration processes, and various incentives are available for businesses, including tax benefits and grants for startups.

Quality of Life: Malta boasts a high quality of life with a pleasant Mediterranean climate, excellent healthcare facilities, and a well-developed education system. English is widely spoken, making it easy for expatriates to integrate into society.

Cost of Living: While Malta offers a high quality of life, it is essential to be aware that the cost of living, especially in popular expat areas like Sliema and St. Julian's, can be relatively high compared to other Mediterranean countries.

Healthcare: Malta has a well-regarded healthcare system, with both public and private options available. Expatriates may opt for private health insurance to access a broader range of services and reduce waiting times.

Education: Malta offers a range of educational institutions, including international schools and universities. Many of these institutions follow English-language curricula, making them suitable for expatriate families.

Cultural Integration: Malta's diverse cultural heritage, influenced by Phoenician, Roman, Arab, and European traditions, provides an enriching experience for those seeking cultural immersion. The Maltese people are known for their warm hospitality and welcoming attitude towards foreigners.

Legal and Financial Considerations: Investors should familiarize themselves with Malta's legal and financial regulations, including tax obligations, property laws, and business registration requirements. Consulting with legal and financial experts is advisable when making significant investments.

Sustainability and Environment: Malta places a growing emphasis on sustainability and environmental conservation. Investors interested in eco-friendly projects may find opportunities in renewable energy, green technologies, and conservation initiatives.

Conclusion: Malta's strategic location, strong economy, and unique Mediterranean lifestyle make it an enticing destination for investors and expatriates. Whether you're considering residency, starting a business, or simply enjoying a new way of life, Malta offers a wealth of opportunities and experiences for those looking to make this charming island their home.

Discovering Hidden Gems: Lesser-Known Attractions

While Malta is celebrated for its famous landmarks and bustling tourist destinations, there is a wealth of lesser-known attractions waiting to be discovered by intrepid travelers. These hidden gems offer a glimpse into the authentic culture, history, and natural beauty of the Maltese Islands.

1. **Ghar Dalam Cave:** Tucked away in the village of Birzebbuga, Ghar Dalam Cave is an archaeological treasure trove. This cave holds evidence of Malta's prehistoric past, with fossils dating back to the Ice Age. It's a fascinating journey through time, showcasing the island's geological and paleontological heritage.

2. **St. Agatha's Tower:** Located in the rural village of Mellieha, this coastal fortification offers panoramic views of the northern coast of Malta. Built by the Knights of St. John, St. Agatha's Tower, also known as the Red Tower, provides an ideal vantage point for watching sunsets and taking in the beauty of the Mediterranean Sea.

3. **The Blue Grotto:** While the Blue Grotto is not entirely hidden, it often remains overshadowed by more famous attractions. This stunning sea cave system on the southwest coast of Malta boasts azure waters and intricate rock formations. Boat tours offer a chance to explore its magical beauty.

4. **Popeye Village:** Nestled in Anchor Bay, this quirky and charming attraction is the original film set of

the 1980 musical production "Popeye." The village is now a theme park, offering visitors a whimsical experience with colorful buildings, a fun water park, and a chance to step into the world of Popeye and his friends.

5. **Hagar Qim and Mnajdra Temples:** These megalithic temples, which predate the pyramids of Egypt, are UNESCO World Heritage Sites and often escape the limelight of their more famous counterparts. Located in Qrendi, they provide a glimpse into Malta's ancient history and are surrounded by a scenic landscape.

6. **Buskett Gardens:** A tranquil escape from the hustle and bustle, Buskett Gardens are a hidden oasis of lush greenery in the heart of Malta. It's the ideal spot for picnics, nature walks, and birdwatching, particularly during the spring and autumn seasons.

7. **Mistra Bay:** This serene bay, located in the northern part of Malta near the town of Mellieha, offers a peaceful retreat away from crowded beaches. Its clear waters are perfect for swimming and snorkeling, and it's an excellent spot to unwind and enjoy the Mediterranean sun.

8. **Dingli Cliffs:** Often overshadowed by the more famous cliffs in Gozo, Dingli Cliffs offer equally breathtaking views of the Mediterranean Sea. The area is known for its tranquility, making it an excellent place for a leisurely hike and a picnic with a view.

9. **Wied il-Ghasri:** A hidden gem on the island of Gozo, Wied il-Ghasri is a narrow gorge leading to a secluded pebble beach. It's an idyllic spot for swimming, snorkeling, and exploring the natural beauty of the Maltese archipelago.

10. **Inland Sea and Azure Window (formerly):**
Although the iconic Azure Window sadly collapsed into the sea, the Inland Sea in Gozo remains an enchanting site. It's a picturesque lagoon surrounded by towering cliffs, and it offers boat trips through a natural tunnel to the open sea.

These hidden gems of Malta and Gozo offer travelers a chance to step off the beaten path and discover the quieter, more authentic side of the islands. Exploring these lesser-known attractions reveals the rich tapestry of history, culture, and natural beauty that make Malta a truly remarkable destination.

Malta's International Relations

In the heart of the Mediterranean, Malta occupies a strategic position that has shaped its international relations throughout history. From its early history as a Phoenician trading post to its current status as a member of the European Union, Malta's international connections have played a pivotal role in its development.

Ancient Roots: Malta's international history dates back to its ancient roots as a crossroads of Mediterranean trade. Phoenician, Roman, Arab, and Byzantine influences left their mark on the island, as traders and conquerors passed through its shores.

Knights of St. John: The Knights Hospitaller, also known as the Knights of St. John, established a presence in Malta in the 16th century. They were granted the island by Emperor Charles V of Spain and used Malta as a stronghold against the Ottoman Empire. Their international network of support and alliances helped Malta withstand sieges and remain a Christian outpost in the Mediterranean.

British Colonial Period: Malta's strategic location caught the eye of the British Empire, and the island became a British colony in the 19th century. It played a crucial role as a naval base during both World Wars, further solidifying its importance on the international stage.

Independence: Malta gained independence from Britain in 1964 and became a republic in 1974. This marked a new era in its international relations, as it sought to establish itself as a sovereign nation. The United Kingdom maintained military bases in Malta until 1979, reflecting the enduring ties between the two nations.

European Union Membership: In 2004, Malta became a full member of the European Union (EU). This move deepened its integration into the international community and provided access to the single European market. It also adopted the euro as its official currency, aligning its economic policies with the EU.

International Diplomacy: Malta maintains diplomatic relations with numerous countries worldwide. Its foreign policy emphasizes peace, stability, and cooperation in the Mediterranean region and beyond. It has also been active in international organizations such as the United Nations and the Commonwealth.

Role in the Mediterranean: As a Mediterranean nation, Malta has taken an active role in addressing regional issues, including migration, maritime security, and environmental concerns. It has hosted international conferences and summits, serving as a bridge between Europe, North Africa, and the Middle East.

International Trade: Malta's open economy relies heavily on international trade, with a focus on services, including finance and tourism. Its strategic location has made it a hub for international business, attracting foreign investment and companies seeking to establish a presence in the EU.

Cultural Diplomacy: Malta's rich cultural heritage is a tool for international diplomacy. It participates in cultural exchanges, promotes its arts and crafts, and hosts international events, such as the Valletta Film Festival and various music and arts festivals.

Humanitarian Efforts: Malta has been involved in humanitarian efforts, including search and rescue operations in the Mediterranean to assist migrants in distress at sea. It has also played a role in peacekeeping missions under the auspices of the United Nations.

Malta's international relations reflect its evolution from an ancient trading post to a modern, sovereign nation actively engaged with the global community. Its strategic location, historic ties, and commitment to diplomacy continue to shape its role in the Mediterranean and beyond.

Maltese Influence on Art and Literature

The Maltese Islands, with their rich history and vibrant culture, have left an indelible mark on the world of art and literature. From ancient civilizations to contemporary creators, Malta's influence has woven its way into the tapestry of human expression.

Ancient Artifacts: Malta's prehistoric temples, such as Hagar Qim and Mnajdra, provide some of the earliest evidence of artistic expression in the Mediterranean. These megalithic structures, dating back to 3600 BC, feature intricate carvings and designs that offer a glimpse into the artistry of Malta's ancient inhabitants.

The Knights of St. John: The arrival of the Knights Hospitaller in the 16th century brought with it a flourishing of artistic endeavors. These knights, many of whom were artists and collectors themselves, patronized the arts and fostered a culture of creativity on the islands. The Grand Masters commissioned elaborate palaces, churches, and artwork, leaving behind a legacy of Baroque and Renaissance masterpieces.

Giuseppe Calì: One of Malta's most celebrated artists, Giuseppe Calì (1846-1930), made significant contributions to the world of art. His works often depicted historical and religious subjects, reflecting his deep connection to Malta's cultural heritage. Calì's paintings are exhibited not only in Malta but also in international collections.

Literary Giants: Malta has also produced literary luminaries who have made their mark on the world stage. Prospero Caffari (1899-1977), a prolific playwright and poet, was known for his evocative and passionate works that explored themes of identity and love. His contributions to Maltese literature are highly regarded.

Dun Karm: Widely hailed as the national poet of Malta, Dun Karm Psaila (1871-1961) holds a revered place in Maltese literature. His poetry, often inspired by the Maltese landscape and culture, played a pivotal role in shaping the nation's identity during its quest for independence. His poem "Innu Malti" (The Maltese Hymn) became the national anthem.

Contemporary Creators: Malta continues to nurture a vibrant arts scene with contemporary artists and authors making waves internationally. The Malta Arts Festival, held annually, showcases a diverse range of artistic expressions, from visual arts to theater, dance, and music. This platform has become a melting pot for both local and international talent.

Artistic Inspiration: Malta's unique geography, with its azure seas, historic cities, and charming villages, has inspired countless artists and writers. The island's cultural diversity, blending elements of North African, European, and Middle Eastern influences, provides a rich tapestry for creative exploration.

Literature and Identity: Maltese literature often grapples with questions of identity, language, and nationhood. The struggle to preserve the Maltese language and foster a distinct literary tradition has been a recurring theme in the works of many Maltese authors.

International Collaborations: Malta's participation in international cultural exchanges, such as the European Capital of Culture program, has further deepened its influence on the global stage. These initiatives have allowed Maltese artists and authors to collaborate with their peers from around the world, enriching the island's creative landscape.

In summary, Malta's influence on art and literature is a testament to its enduring cultural legacy. From its prehistoric temples to the contemporary works of its artists and authors, Malta continues to inspire and captivate the world with its unique blend of history, culture, and artistic expression.

Preserving Malta's Cultural Heritage

Malta, with its storied past and rich cultural tapestry, stands as a testament to the enduring legacy of human civilization. In this chapter, we delve into the tireless efforts and initiatives aimed at preserving Malta's remarkable cultural heritage.

Heritage Sites: At the heart of Malta's preservation efforts lie its numerous heritage sites. The archipelago boasts an impressive array of historical, archaeological, and architectural treasures. These sites, including the megalithic temples, fortifications, and medieval cities, have been meticulously conserved and recognized as UNESCO World Heritage Sites. The commitment to safeguarding these treasures for future generations is paramount.

Restoration Projects: Over the years, Malta has undertaken extensive restoration projects to breathe new life into its historic structures. The restoration of Valletta, Malta's capital, is a prime example. The meticulous restoration of the city's Baroque architecture and fortifications earned it a UNESCO World Heritage designation. Such efforts ensure that these architectural marvels remain a vibrant part of Malta's cultural landscape.

Museums and Cultural Institutions: Malta is home to a diverse range of museums and cultural institutions that play a pivotal role in preserving the nation's heritage. The National Museum of Archaeology, housed in the Auberge de Provence, showcases Malta's prehistoric and classical past. The Malta Maritime Museum, located in Vittoriosa, celebrates the island's maritime history. These institutions serve as custodians of Malta's cultural treasures, offering insights into its rich history.

Language Preservation: The Maltese language, with its Semitic and Romance influences, is an integral part of the nation's identity. Efforts to preserve and promote the Maltese language are evident in educational initiatives and language policies. Maltese and English are both official languages, ensuring that the Maltese language remains a vibrant and evolving aspect of the nation's culture.

Folklore and Traditions: Malta's cultural heritage is also alive in its folklore and traditions. Festivals like the Festa season, celebrating the patron saints of various towns and villages, offer a glimpse into the island's deep-rooted religious and community traditions. Folklore, passed down through generations, continues to shape the cultural identity of Malta.

Cultural Events: The Maltese calendar is dotted with cultural events that celebrate its heritage. These events range from traditional music and dance festivals to art exhibitions and historical reenactments. The Malta International Arts Festival and the Malta Jazz Festival are among the prominent events that showcase the island's vibrant cultural scene.

Education and Awareness: Malta places a strong emphasis on education and awareness when it comes to preserving its cultural heritage. Schools and institutions actively promote the appreciation of Maltese history, language, and traditions among the younger generation. This ensures that the legacy of Malta's cultural heritage is carried forward.

International Collaborations: Malta actively collaborates with international organizations and partners in the field of cultural heritage preservation. The island's participation in initiatives like the European Capital of Culture and the European Heritage Days fosters cultural exchange and highlights Malta's commitment to preserving its unique identity.

In conclusion, Malta's dedication to preserving its cultural heritage is evident in its meticulous efforts to protect historic sites, restore architectural marvels, promote its language, and celebrate its traditions. This unwavering commitment ensures that Malta's rich and diverse cultural legacy continues to flourish and enchant generations to come.

Maltese Innovations and Achievements

Malta, often celebrated for its historical and cultural significance, has also made notable contributions to the world of innovation and achievement. In this chapter, we'll explore some of the remarkable accomplishments and innovations associated with the Maltese people.

1. George Abela and Medical Research: George Abela, a Maltese doctor and researcher, has made significant contributions to the field of medical research. His work in cancer research, particularly on the role of vitamin D in preventing cancer, has garnered international attention. His efforts have paved the way for a better understanding of cancer prevention and treatment.

2. Malta's Role in Blockchain Technology: Malta has earned a reputation as the "Blockchain Island" due to its progressive stance on blockchain technology and cryptocurrencies. The government's proactive approach in creating a regulatory framework for blockchain companies has attracted blockchain innovators and businesses from around the world. This has positioned Malta as a hub for blockchain development and innovation.

3. Medicine and Healthcare: Malta has a well-established healthcare system that has produced accomplished medical professionals and researchers. Notable Maltese physicians and scientists have made strides in various fields, including cardiology, neurology, and genetics. Their contributions to medical research and patient care have received recognition at the international level.

4. Astronomy and Space Exploration: The Maltese Islands have been home to passionate astronomers who have made notable contributions to the field of space exploration. The Maltese Association of Astronomy, led by Dr. Richard Zrinzo, has actively promoted astronomy education and research. Malta's geographic location also makes it an ideal spot for stargazing and astronomical observations.

5. Sustainable Energy: Malta has been actively exploring sustainable energy solutions to address environmental challenges. The country's commitment to renewable energy sources, such as solar and wind power, has led to the development of innovative technologies and practices in the energy sector. These efforts contribute to Malta's sustainability goals and reduce its carbon footprint.

6. Aviation and Aerospace: Maltese individuals have made advancements in aviation and aerospace. Malta's role as a strategic location in the Mediterranean has been historically significant for aviation during times of conflict. Today, the island hosts aviation companies engaged in aircraft maintenance, repair, and servicing, contributing to the global aerospace industry.

7. Film Industry: Malta's film industry has garnered recognition on the international stage. The country's diverse landscapes and historic sites have attracted filmmakers from Hollywood and beyond. Films like "Gladiator" and "Game of Thrones" have been shot in Malta, showcasing its versatility as a location for cinematic productions.

8. Philanthropy and Social Innovation: Maltese individuals and organizations have a long history of philanthropy and social innovation. The Malta Community Chest Fund Foundation, under the patronage of the President of Malta, is an example of a charitable organization that supports various social causes and initiatives.

9. Entrepreneurship and Startups: Malta has seen a surge in entrepreneurship and startups, with a focus on technology and innovation. The government's support for startups and the presence of incubators and accelerators have nurtured a thriving ecosystem for innovation and business development.

In conclusion, Malta's contributions to innovation and achievements span a diverse range of fields, from medical research and technology to sustainability and the arts. The island's dedication to fostering a culture of innovation and progress continues to shape its role on the global stage.

Planning Your Visit to Malta

As you embark on the exciting journey of planning your visit to Malta, you're about to discover a Mediterranean gem that seamlessly combines history, culture, natural beauty, and warm hospitality. This chapter serves as your comprehensive guide to ensuring that your trip to Malta is an unforgettable experience.

1. Visa and Entry Requirements: Before you pack your bags, make sure you understand Malta's entry requirements. Most visitors from European Union (EU) countries can enter Malta with just their passport or identity card. Non-EU citizens may need a visa, so check the official government website for the latest information.

2. Best Time to Visit: Malta enjoys a Mediterranean climate with hot, dry summers and mild winters. The best time to visit is typically during the spring (April to June) and autumn (September to October) when the weather is pleasant, and the crowds are thinner. Summer (July and August) is high season, attracting sunseekers and beach lovers.

3. Accommodation: Malta offers a wide range of accommodation options to suit every budget and preference. You'll find luxury hotels, boutique guesthouses, charming bed-and-breakfasts, and self-catering apartments. Be sure to book your accommodations well in advance, especially during peak tourist seasons.

4. Transportation: Getting around Malta is relatively easy. The island has a well-developed public transportation system, including buses and ferries. Taxis and car rentals are also readily available. If you plan to explore the sister islands of Gozo and Comino, ferries are the most convenient mode of transport.

5. Currency and Payment: The currency used in Malta is the Euro (EUR). Credit cards are widely accepted in hotels, restaurants, and shops. However, it's a good idea to carry some cash for small purchases and in case you visit more remote areas.

6. Language: While English and Maltese are both official languages, you'll find that English is widely spoken and understood, making communication easy for most visitors.

7. Safety: Malta is considered a safe destination for travelers. The crime rate is low, and the locals are known for their friendliness and helpfulness. Nevertheless, it's always wise to take basic safety precautions, such as safeguarding your belongings.

8. Local Cuisine: Maltese cuisine is a delectable blend of Mediterranean flavors. Be sure to try traditional dishes like pastizzi (savory pastries), rabbit stew, and ftira (a type of Maltese bread). And don't forget to pair your meals with local wines, which are known for their unique character.

9. Cultural Etiquette: When visiting churches and religious sites, it's customary to dress modestly, covering shoulders and knees. Tipping is appreciated but not obligatory. A 10% tip in restaurants is common practice.

10. Must-See Attractions: Malta boasts a wealth of historical and cultural attractions, including the UNESCO World Heritage-listed city of Valletta, the ancient temples of Hagar Qim and Mnajdra, the medieval town of Mdina, and the Blue Grotto. Comino's Blue Lagoon and Gozo's Azure Window are also must-visit natural wonders.

11. Tours and Activities: Consider joining guided tours to make the most of your visit. You can explore historical sites, take boat trips to the Blue Grotto, or even embark on scuba diving adventures to discover Malta's underwater world.

12. Festivals and Events: Check the local event calendar for festivals and events happening during your visit. The Festa season, Carnival, and the Malta International Arts Festival are just a few of the vibrant celebrations you might encounter.

13. Souvenirs: Don't forget to pick up some souvenirs to remember your trip by. Maltese lace, glassware, and handmade crafts are popular choices.

With these essential tips in mind, you're well-prepared to plan your visit to Malta. Whether you're drawn to the island's rich history, stunning landscapes, or vibrant culture, Malta promises a memorable experience that will leave you with cherished memories for years to come.

Epilogue

As we conclude our journey through the vibrant and diverse world of Malta, it's worth reflecting on the rich tapestry of experiences, history, and culture we've explored together. Malta, with its ancient origins dating back to prehistoric times, has left an indelible mark on the Mediterranean and the hearts of those who visit.

From the awe-inspiring Neolithic temples of Hagar Qim and Mnajdra to the grandeur of Valletta, a city that stands as a testament to the Knights of St. John's legacy, Malta's historical significance is profound. The Arab, Byzantine, and Roman influences that shaped this archipelago are evident in its architecture, language, and traditions.

We've marveled at the natural wonders, from the enchanting Blue Grotto to the crystal-clear waters of the Blue Lagoon on the island of Comino. We've tasted the flavors of Malta through its delectable cuisine, a delightful fusion of Mediterranean ingredients and culinary traditions.

The vibrant festivals and celebrations, rooted in deep-seated traditions and folklore, have provided insight into the Maltese way of life, where community and heritage are celebrated with fervor.

Malta's role in World War II, as a bastion of resilience and courage in the face of adversity, is a testament to the island's enduring spirit. We've explored the contemporary landscape, understanding the challenges and opportunities that shape Malta today.

This island nation has also showcased its commitment to sustainability in tourism and its dedication to preserving its cultural heritage. The innovative achievements of the Maltese people have not gone unnoticed, demonstrating their determination to make a global impact.

As we conclude our journey through the pages of this book, I encourage you to embark on your own adventure to Malta, a place where history meets the modern world, and where the warmth of its people matches the Mediterranean sun. Whether you're an intrepid traveler, a history enthusiast, or simply seeking a tranquil escape, Malta has something to offer everyone.

May your exploration of this remarkable archipelago be filled with unforgettable moments, cultural discoveries, and the joy of making new memories. As you venture forth to discover Malta's hidden gems, may your experiences be as unique and rewarding as the island itself.